P9-DFV-643

SIGNS and WONDERS

WITHDRAWN

134768

Richard B. Wilke

SIGNS and WONDERS

The Mighty Work of God in the Church

ABINGDON PRESS
NASHVILLE

134768

SIGNS AND WONDERS

Copyright © 1989 by Abingdon Press

Third Printing 1990

All rights reserved.
No part of this work may be reproduced or transmitted in any form or by any means, electronic or mechanical, including photocopying and recording, or by any information storage or retrieval system, except as may be expressly permitted by the 1976 Copyright Act or in writing from the publisher. Requests for permission should be addressed in writing to Abingdon Press, 201 Eighth Avenue South, Nashville, TN 37202.

This book is printed on acid-free paper.

Library of Congress Cataloging-in-Publication Data

Wilke, Richard B., 1930–
  Signs and wonders.
  1. Church renewal. 2. Christianity—20th century. 3. Holy Spirit.
I. Title.
BV600.2.W535   1989   262'.001'7   89-45535

ISBN 0-687-38448-6 (alk. paper)

Scripture quotations, unless otherwise noted, are from the Revised Standard Version of the Bible, copyright 1946, 1952, 1971 by the Division of Christian Education of the National Council of Churches of Christ in the USA. Used by permission.

Those noted GNB are from the *Good News Bible*—Old Testament: Copyright © American Bible Society 1976; New Testament: Copyright © American Bible Society 1966, 1971, 1976. Used by permission.

Those noted KJV are from the King James Version of the Bible.

The poem "I Stand By the Door" by Samuel Shoemaker is from *I Stand By the Door* by Helen Smith Shoemaker. Copyright © 1967 by Word Books, Dallas, Texas. Used by permission.

The excerpt from the poem "Sic Transit" by Sara Henderson Hay is from *Field of Honor* by Sara Henderson Hay. Copyright © 1933 by Sara Henderson Hay. Used by permission of the Sara Henderson Hay Collection, Carnegie Mellon University Libraries, Pittsburgh, Pennsylvania.

MANUFACTURED IN THE UNITED STATES OF AMERICA

To Stephen and Beth, Paul and Janelle, Susan, and Sarah—my
children—who in their ministries show signs and wonders of a
church reborn.

In appreciation to:

Margaret Ault, manuscript preparation
Greg Michael, Abingdon Press editor
Julia Wilke, love and encouragement

See how great a flame aspires,
Kindled by a spark of grace!
Jesus' love the nations fires,
Sets the kingdoms on a blaze.
To bring fire on earth he came;
Kindled in some hearts it is:
O that all might catch the flame,
All partake the glorious bliss!

When he first the work begun,
Small and feeble was his day.
Now the Word doth swiftly run;
Now it wins its widening way;
More and more it spreads and grows,
Ever mighty to prevail;
Sin's strongholds it now o'erthrows,
Shakes the trembling gates of hell.

Sons of God your Savior praise,
He the door hath opened wide;
He hath given the word of grace;
Jesus' word is glorified.
Jesus mighty to redeem,
He alone the work hath wrought;
Worthy is the work of him,
Him who spake a world from naught.

Saw ye not the cloud arise,
Little as a human hand?
Now it spreads along the skies,
Hangs o'er all the thirsty land;
Lo! the promise of a shower
Drops already from above;
But the Lord will shortly pour
All the spirit of his love.

Charles Wesley

CONTENTS

CHAPTER ONE

Signs and Wonders

Sang Kyoo Lee and his wife, Young Gum, stepped confidently into my office. Young Gum beamed, her eyes flashing like coals of fire. You would have thought I was interviewing an engaged couple about to be married rather than a preacher ready to start a new church.

"We have been praying for one hundred nights—one, two hours every night—asking God to give us power and victory," Sang Kyoo began.

"Yes," Young Gum seconded. "Every night, faithfully for one hundred nights. We have been praying before coming to see you."

"We believe God wants us to begin new work with Koreans in Arkansas," said Sang Kyoo. "And we need much power."

Although I was taken aback by their spiritual intensity, I was not completely unprepared for what they told me. I knew that five years before, in the Mok Yang Methodist Church in Seoul, Korea, where Sang's brother-in-law was pastor, Sang was lay leader. During prayers in a morning worship service, Sang Kyoo and Young Gum had stepped forward and offered themselves before Reverend Sang Kil Bae to enter the ministry. I knew about the hardships of bringing two children to the United States—struggling with the English language, financial problems, and finally completing seminary.

"We don't have many Koreans in Central Arkansas, do we?" I asked.

"Oh, yes," Sang Kyoo replied. "We think as many as three or four hundred. We can travel fifty miles in every direction and make class meetings in different towns."

"They aren't Christians, are they?" I asked.

"No, not most, but we must lead them to Christ," he answered. "We will hold Sunday afternoon worship in First Church, Jacksonville. Also, Friday night prayers and Saturday Bible study."

"What about your support?"

"The district superintendent promised us $1,000 each month and a house."

My administrative hat told me that included travel, utilities—the works—not up to our minimum support, and he was a deacon on probation, too. I must look into that.

Then my thoughts raced back to Barnabas, who sold his farm in Cyprus, and took everything he had to Jerusalem, laying it at Peter's feet.

"Let us all know when you hold your first worship service," I commented, a bit too casually.

"Our first worship service will be the day we move into the parsonage. My wife, Young Gum, son, John, daughter, Susan, and I will kneel down and pray." Then he gave a big smile of confidence, "We'll have a congregation of four," he said, lifting up four fingers.

My heart beat faster. Their spirit was contagious. I kept thinking of practical things, like a refrigerator and clothes for the children and automobile tires, so I asked, "Is there anything at all I can do to help?"

They both rose as one and said, "Oh, yes, there is." They paused, as if afraid to ask. "Would you pray for us? We will need much power."

We held hands in that tiny circle of three and prayed for power. In my mind's eye, I saw the converts they would make. I envisioned a Korean congregation that would rise up out of nowhere, like the early Christians at Antioch.

I decided to take off my black arm band. The church is not dead yet.

Looking and Listening

Lately I've been listening to the churches. In pastors' schools and annual conferences, in workshops on church growth and discipleship, I've been visiting with pastors and church leaders from coast to coast. Plucked out of the parish, I've now been freed to go here and there, even into other parts of the world, watching in amazement the signs and wonders of God's mighty works.

Now I'm less like a soldier in the field and more like a war correspondent surveying the struggle. Sometimes I've felt like the spies Moses sent into Canaan to survey the scene and bring back a report, or like the dove Noah kept dispatching to learn whether the storm was over.

I wrote the book *And Are We Yet Alive?* to be a journalistic scream in the night. I figured that only a few church leaders would read the precipitous decline of major denominations. Imagine my surprise at the stir it created among laity as well as ministers. Even other denominations got involved. One general superintendent of the Church of the Nazarene thanked me and said, "I fear that we are only a few years behind you."

Top writers and leaders of large churches plunged into the discussion with vigor. Bishop Earl G. Hunt, Jr., while president of the Council of Bishops, wrote *A Bishop Speaks His Mind*. It was no small thing for him to say, "Something is deeply wrong . . . within all of mainstream Protestantism. . . . We are hiding our lights under a bushel of structure."

William H. Willimon and Robert L. Wilson, in *Rekindling the Flame*, point to a crisis of structure and strategy in The United Methodist Church "unequaled since the schism preceding the Civil War."

George G. Hunter III made a brilliant comparison of John Wesley's revival to modern church growth strategies in *To Spread the Power*. Wesley focused on the unchurched and understood how to develop group life for growing Christians—approaches to growth recommended today.

Douglas Johnson and Alan Waltz wrote *Facts and Possibilities*, pointing to the inordinate energy expended on the organization. The major task for the future "must be the strengthening of the ministries in the local church."

Response

When *And Are We Yet Alive?* came out, Abingdon Press urged people to write, and write they did. Hundreds of long, late-at-night letters came in response.

Some people told of exciting new Sunday school classes, new choirs, witnessing teams, and calling programs they were forming. One lady in Ohio wrote, "You will be pleased. I am presently a part of a growing church. We have all kinds of mission programs, distributing food, visiting nursing homes, support groups. Classes and prayer groups are provided all through the week. The Kingdom of God is breaking through. Emphasis is never on numbers for numbers' sake, but on persons . . . and the church is growing."

A woman who pastors in Minnesota is full of enthusiasm. "We have a support group for divorced people, for bereavement, a fellowship group for singles, active visitation by laypeople and pastors. We are growing."

Several told of their call to ministry. A woman in Vermont said, "You will be interested to know that my pastor is just beginning with the 'cell group' plan, and in a very small rural town he presently has over forty people involved weekly in a lay leadership Bible series. Our group of ten has grown four times, several who were not churchgoing people. I have personally observed people grow in their relationship with our Living Lord and Savior. I have been called into the [ordained] ministry at age forty-four."

Some seminarians were encouraged. A young man wrote from North Carolina: "I am only into your book, but I have so much on my heart because of it. I am a senior student in seminary and so green that I wouldn't burn, but there is a fire burning in my belly that expects me to give my best in order to praise God."

A number of letters were critical of their churches. One lady said it was too late. "In 1984, I became a statistic," she said.

"My greatest disappointment in the church," says a Missouri pastor, "is that the agenda is always 'business as usual.' "

A minister in Kentucky says, "The only way I can operate without frustration and depression is to ignore the rest of the denomination."

Some of the criticism was constructive. "I've considered many times leaving this dead denomination," wrote a layman from Maine. "We house the local food bank, but we don't offer Christ to people in need, particularly the poor. We only preach to the converted."

Some correspondents made helpful suggestions. A minister to singles in Georgia hit hard: "With almost one-half the adult population being single, I cannot imagine how we could even think of stopping our membership decline without a very intentional effort at singles ministry."

A director of Christian education in Florida realizes that her church plans programs that "fit best into the custodian's schedule."

Even more poignant is what a minister from New Jersey wrote: "I finished your book feeling inadequate as a pastor. Presently I am serving a typical congregation of over 300 members, composed of persons whose average age is 60 +. It is a very stable community. The members have come to expect personal caring from the pastor in the form of visitation, serving the sacraments, and grief/emergency counseling. In addition, much of the daily administration of the budget and building is done from the church office. Less than 1 percent of my time has been spent in building up the congregation." Then he asked the big question: "How can I move from pastor to trainer?"

A few letters made me shout "Halleluia." A preacher's daughter in Louisiana decided that "latchkey care" for teenaged girls was not good enough. She meets with them after school to study the Bible, to have prayer, and to help them find Christ.

But the letter I received most often always made me smile with appreciation: "I have been thinking your thoughts for some time."

The Bad News

My friends gave me two sets of warnings as I prepared to write this book. The first pleaded, "Don't lead us in another litany of denominational decline. We are tired of hearing bad news about the church. We have been flagellating ourselves long enough."

The other group insisted, "Wilke, we are counting on you to tell the truth. Don't sidestep any harsh realities." We are not helped when the harshest critics soften their blows.

So, we'll say it straight, but we'll say it fast. Here are the facts.

I received the letter on a gray drizzling Friday afternoon in late November. Warren Hartman, longtime observer of membership patterns for The United Methodist Church and statistician for the Board of Discipleship, tried to hide his disappointment, but he gave me the latest figures.

Quietly and unassumingly, The United Methodist Church in the United States will slip out of the nine million member category into the eight million category this year. It's only symbolic, I know—no more severe than any other week or month or year. But it hit me like a ton of bricks.

In spite of hard work by many, the report for 1987 showed a severe decline in membership from 9,082,790 to 9,006,721. Losing about 76,000 members in 1987 means that little has changed. Each year, the denomination declines 65,000 to 80,000, each week about 1,470, or about six "average" 250 member churches a week. I calculate that somewhere between February 5 and 15, 1988 the downward speedometer turned over another million. That means we dropped from having 11 million members in the 1960s to 10 million members in the 1970s, to 9 million members in the 1980s, to the now 8 million member category as we prepare for the 1990s. The full experience for 1988 promises to be equally severe, for it was the quadrennial year of conferences—annual, jurisdictional, general—requiring a vast expenditure of energy on internal affairs.

Hartman, ever the optimist, points to a hopeful sign or two. The number of baptisms increased by 727, the preparatory roll (baptized children) grew by 5,899, and the constituency roll (friends, inquirers, interested persons) moved up by 16,885.

The figures are still unofficial, but they are based on experience and are reliably accurate. Can you believe that our statistics on membership (not finances) take over a year to be compiled? And no one in a leadership role is responsible for holding the system accountable. Is anybody there? Does anybody care? Hartman's chart is on page 17.

Line Item

Membership	9,082,790	9,012,604	− 76,069	− 0.77
(Loss the year before was 67,878)				
Worship Attn.	3,486,114	3,449,437	− 39,603	− 1.05
(Loss the year before was 17,372)				
Conf. Faith	194,448	186,318	− 8,006	− 4.18
Baptisms	179,264	179,991	+ 727	+ 0.4
Prep. Roll	1,360,954	1,368,661	+ 5,899	+ 0.4
Constit. Roll	1,226,424	1,243,309	+ 16,885	+ 1.4
Conf. Class	127,406	120,525	− 6,881	− 5.4
Ch. School Mbrs.	3,943,353	3,926,610	− 19,872	− 0.5
SS Attendance	1,986,670	1,975,610	− 59,061	− 0.56

Most discouraging, in spite of strong efforts in several quarters, are the drop in Sunday school membership by nearly 20,000 and the drop in Sunday school attendance, a more accurate figure, by nearly 60,000. Given the reality that for over a century Sunday school attendance has a three-year "lead time" over church membership, we still are in a downward spiral.

Some experts in church growth, such as Win Arn and Lyle Schaller, question my constant concern with the Sunday school. They emphasize worship. So, from their perspective, the over 35,000 decline in worship attendance denotes another severe negative.

This decline occurs amid increased population expansion. The population goes up; the membership goes down. In 1968, the United Methodists comprised 6 percent of the country's population; in 1988, less than 4 percent.

Other mainline national denominations—such as the Christian Church (Disciples of Christ), the Episcopalians, and the Presbyterians—continue to decline at the same undisturbed pace. The United Church of Christ, as we will see later, has applied the brakes but is still declining.

Faith Reaffirmed

Why does this negative news not lead me to despair? Why am I more excited about the church's ministry than ever before? Let me explain.

I am filled with hope and excitement because I have met many people who are alive in Christ. I have visited many churches that quiver with excitement. I have talked with many pastors and lay leaders who are working and praying for revitalization of local congregations and denominational structures.

Many people in churches across the land wonder and they worry. Is the church dying? Are we without hope? The word to them must be the word God gave Elijah when Elijah feared he was all alone. God rebuked Elijah: "I will leave seven thousand in Israel, all the knees that have not bowed to Baal" (I Kings 19:18). You are not alone. Time would fail me to tell of all the signs and wonders that God is performing all over the world.

I was surprised to discover so many congregations, in nice rhythm, moving like a pendulum into the Word, then out into the world. The danger with statistics is that they average everything, forgetting the local, the unique, and the special. One business expert, commenting on a recent recession, said, "It's not fair to say the country had a recession. Rather, some states had a recession; some states had a boom. Some manufacturing plants closed, some expanded." So it is with the church. National averages may not describe the degree of spiritual heat in your congregation.

John W. Gardner, in *Self Renewal*, put revitalization of institutions into proper perspective.

> Our thinking about growth and decay is dominated by the image of a single life-span, animal or vegetable. Seedling, full flower, and death. 'The flower that once has blown forever dies.' But for an ever-renewing society the appropriate image is a total garden, a balanced aquarium or other ecological system. Some things are dying—but the system lives on.

A denomination is like a garden. Some flowers are fading; some are blooming. I have walked into worship services I hated to leave. I have listened to young people testify to the saving work of Christ in their hearts. I have watched people go to Haiti at their own expense to drill water wells, doctors travel to Honduras to perform surgery, kids bus their way to Appalachia to paint houses. I have observed churches reaching out with friendship and caring to people with handicapping conditions, to single adults, and to minorities. Statistics never tell the whole story.

I have seen faithful pastors of evangelical congregations in areas of declining populations convert, baptize, and nurture, even as another family vacates the farm or a dozen members leave town when the plant closes. Never have I been more convinced that our task is to be faithful, to make disciples, not just to "grow a church." At the same time I refuse to let off the hook churches who complain about economic conditions and allow people to perish only blocks from the sanctuary.

Authentic vitality seems to pulsate where a congregation is most in harmony with the apostolic witness. The early Christians knew that their lives had been changed. They were able to share their experiences so that others could become followers. The apostles focused on preaching, teaching, healing, and prayer. Churches that use helium balloons or live camels in the Christmas pageant or strobe lights on the pulpit do not hold the key. Authentic biblical Christianity is working. Look for signs of life, and you will generally find honest, straightforward New Testament Christianity. "And with great power the apostles gave their testimony to the resurrection of the Lord Jesus, and great grace was upon them all" (Acts 4:33).

Even troubles in the churches have strengthened my faith in God. Some congregations have no converting power because of a mean attitude. Others are so filled with strife that all their energies are consumed with internal bickering. Some congregations are so proud, so pompous, and so complacent that newcomers cannot get in. Jesus has promised that the Father will prune these churches. God is at work.

"Every branch of mine that bears no fruit, he takes away," said Jesus (John 15:2). Instead of bemoaning the fact that some congregations are "dying on the vine," we ought to rejoice that the Word of God stands bold and true altogether. The disciples were aghast when Jesus cursed the fig tree because it bore no fruit (Matt. 21:19). We, too, stand amazed. But should we not also be filled with wonder and awe that the Savior's promises are eternally true? Whole denominations will be pruned if they do not reproduce.

A prominent preacher and friend of mine gave rebuttal to *And Are We Yet Alive?* He insisted that our task is not to grow, but "to be faithful." I agree that we are not called to be "successful," but, without being argumentative, my question is what are we to be faithful to? Are we not to be faithful to the command of Jesus, "Go . . . make disciples" (Matt. 28:19)?

My faith in God is also strengthened when I consider recent exposés of some of the TV evangelists. I do not rejoice in their trouble any more than I celebrate the scandal of a prominent pastor. But I do make two observations. First, neither the bankruptcy of PTL nor the defrocking of Jimmy Swaggart has appreciably influenced the membership of local churches. That intrigues me. It says to me that local congregations hold the primary spiritual power. Face-to-face relationships still contain the strengths of saving grace. Faithful local pastors, armed with integrity and grace, hold the people's respect. The battles of life are being won or lost in the trenches by the local congregation.

The second observation is a bit like the awful judgment of God upon the branches that didn't bear fruit. We are warned by Jesus "to be aware of covetousness" (Luke 12:15). In the name of money, all sorts of sins can spring forth, for "the love of money is the root of all evils" (I Tim. 6:10). The Bible is still telling the truth.

Sexual promiscuity is the enemy of the faith; yet, it nips at the church every day in a thousand ways. When church leaders in high places fall, the sound is like a giant tree crashing in the forest. Late night talk show host Johnny Carson knocked me off my chair one night when, after another "make fun of" reference to Jim and Tammy Bakker, he suggested that with the downfall of the TV evangelists, even atheists were beginning to believe in God.

The judgments of God should help us believe scriptural promises all the more. We are relearning that the God of the Bible still drops his plumb line to measure the straightness of the church.

Then, too, I'm proud of our efforts to work with churches in the ecumenical movement. Our Lord's final "priestly" prayer asked the Father "that they may be one so that the world might believe." John Wesley looked for comrades, offensive and defensive, in the fight against the devil. Our efforts for social justice, our intentionality to be inclusive racially and culturally, our joy in receiving women in places of leadership, including the pastorate, are great spiritual victories. Johnson and Waltz are correct. These efforts, including the structural housekeeping involved, have consumed our finances and our energy. Yet, I'm glad we addressed these concerns. Some denominations that are currently growing must someday face those same issues. If we are to be the church, we must maintain internal integrity.

Still, I refuse to fall into the trap of those self-satisfied saints who say that we should be content to be a righteous remnant without trying to make new disciples. They point with pride to other ministries. However, our faults are not in our victories but in our failures. To paraphrase Jesus, "These things you ought to have done without neglecting the weightier matters" (see Matt. 23:23). We should not have lost our evangelistic thrust. The good news is that many congregations have not. We observe signs of spiritual vitality and growth all around the world, and we can say with excitement "lo here" and "lo there"!

Growing Churches

What would be the best way to discover dynamics of growth? The Membership Growth Committee of The United Methodist Church, which I chaired, asked a cross-section of pastors of growing churches to come together to share their experiences.

Sixty pastors, young and old, men and women of all races gathered together from all over the United States. They represented all sizes and types of churches, from a three-point charge in North Carolina to a Texas church with thousands of members. Some churches were new, like a fledgling congregation in Florida. Some were established congregations, like a downtown church in Minneapolis. Ethnic churches included black congregations in Harlem and Kansas City.

What are these leaders like?

First, they know "where they are." They ask questions: "Why did God put our church in this part of San Francisco or Atlanta? What is our purpose in being here? What does God want us to do?" They are intentional in their response to a unique local setting.

Second, they have a vision. One observer said, "Some of these pastors have gone to churches that had no vision and have helped create one. Others have seen the visions of their people and have become cheerleaders."

Third, they are flexible and are not limited by outside structures or authority that says, "This is the way you ought to run your church." Sometimes they bend the rules in order to get the job done. They are pragmatists. If it works, they do it; if it doesn't work, they stop doing it. They are not afraid to swipe ideas from others.

Fourth, they are good managers. They spend their time where it will do the most good. They consider preaching to be a top priority, so they will spend time to make sure it goes right. They are attentive to their families and to their physical and spiritual health. They see the lack of enthusiasm as a major problem. "If you are tired, beaten down, exhausted, you cannot be an enthusiastic leader." They are hard workers, not workaholics.

I asked what was important to them. Overwhelmingly, worship was tops. Visitors touch the hem of the garment of Christ on Sunday morning. Sunday worship is exciting to them, and they want it to be exciting for their congregations. They try to preach with passion. They want the people to sing with enthusiasm and pray with power.

They agreed that body-life of the congregation held and nurtured people. Strong advocates of the Sunday school, they also developed missional task forces, special study groups, choirs, and day classes. They work hard to create a place for everyone to be in ministry. Much pastoral care is translated into formation of group life.

These pastors are constantly developing new ministries with lay leadership. They readily delegate to others and release hands on control, but they stress accountability.

The average tenure in their pastorates is 6.9 years, whereas the overall average in most denominations is about 3.2 years. It takes time to grow a church. They emphasized a "pastor-congregational" fit and the need for long-term ministries. One pastor said, "My ministry began to take off after the fifth year."

An exciting development was the formation of "Growth-Plus Associates," led by Dr. Joe Harding. "Growth-Plus" took these pastors, added several hundred others, and trained them to apply growth dynamics with biblical integrity. Then, in a one-to-one arrangement, these pastors agreed to serve as "consultants" to one another and to other churches, giving valuable outside help in strengthening the church's ministry.

Two Case Studies

Protestants across the United States have boarded up or sold half their downtown city churches since World War II. Half of the remainder are on their way out. An archbishop in the Roman Catholic Church is trying to shut down many inner-city churches in Detroit. It's tough to be effective in downtown metropolitan areas.

White Temple Methodist Episcopal and Trinity Methodist Episcopal, South, merged to form First Church, Miami, Florida, in 1966, only to have their properties bought up in the seventies by the city. Most members were moving to the suburbs. A faithful remnant courageously voted to stay downtown. They decided to use their money for a modest, but modern, new structure in the heart of Miami to minister to the needs of the people of the city.

They are a mission-minded bunch of Christians, serving juice, doughnuts, and coffee at "The Breakfast Club" early Sunday mornings for street people. They share devotions, friendship, and Bible study.

Fellowship with the street people—mostly young men whose brains have been scorched by drugs or alcohol—was strengthened by a day of choose-up-sides softball with T-shirts, caps, and hot dogs. Pastor Bill Barnes claims that "everybody won."

This congregation carried tons of food right past other churches to Belle Glade, where Haitian and Jamaican farm

workers cut cane. It is reported that this is the highest per
capita AIDS population in the United States. When the healthy
workers move on to pick Georgia peaches and New York
apples, they leave their children, women, and the sick and
weaker ones behind. First Church goes into action with a
ministry of medicine, clothing, and food.

What surprised me most about this church was that it is
growing. In the middle of a commercial area across from the
docks where you depart to take Caribbean cruises, near the
crime-ridden locale of "Miami Vice," this congregation is
making new converts and is receiving new members.

How? Top pastoral leadership holds the old-timers steady
and attracts new members who want to be in hands-on ministry. A Spanish-speaking, mostly Cuban, wing of the church
holds Sunday school and morning and evening worship with
Reverend Eleazar Legra. Some of their English-speaking
children go to the Anglo Sunday school and worship service and
sing in the choirs.

But even more growth is coming from other areas. English-
speaking people from Jamaica and other Caribbean Islands and
a few English-speaking Hispanics have joined the fellowship.
Several people who had been on drugs and alcohol have come
into the fellowship. Some singles claim the fellowship. Some
committed yuppies are joining the cause. Don't be surprised to
see a Jamaican clapping after a solo or a Hispanic charismatic
lifting a hand during the prayer or a former Episcopalian
crossing herself or himself on entering the pew.

Now look at Wesley United Methodist Church, also in
Miami. Wesley was originally an English-speaking church. It
has been changing since Cuban immigrants have arrived in the
area. The Reverend Deborah McLeod pastors the English-
speaking congregation, and the Reverend Benita Acebo serves
the Spanish-speaking congregation. About 40 people worship
with Wesley; about 175 worship with Iglesia Wesley. In a few
years, the church may become a large, totally Spanish-speaking
congregation.

But here's the point. The congregations now happily share
the facilities. Both English-speaking and Spanish-speaking
people serve on the board of trustees. The growing Spanish-

speaking congregation has provided large gifts of money to remodel the church. The old-timers at Wesley, at their own volition, have given an undivided half interest of their church to the emerging Hispanic fellowship. That reflects life in the city. That exhibits Christianity in the middle of it all, when the Spirit is willing to keep the witness alive.

Around the Country

What about areas of major growth? Not even hundreds of individual congregations that are growing can turn around an entire denomination. What is being achieved in conferences and areas? Let's look at the larger picture.

Bishop Felton May spends a day with confirmands from all over his episcopal area. That act encourages each pastor to have classes and underlines for each youth the importance of his or her Christian commitment.

Churches in states like Virginia, Illinois, Florida, California, Wisconsin, New Jersey, and Texas are stepping up new church starts, including work among minorities. Many areas are experimenting with evangelism strategies. In a program called "South Dakota Grow," seventeen churches worked together to achieve 15 percent growth in 1987. Southwest Texas has developed a concerted conference program using outside consultants on church growth.

I was present when Bishop Jack Tuell ordained the first Vietnamese United Methodist elder in the United States. Another small breakthrough, demonstrating an awareness of the new ethnic groups. It's happening—slowly, haltingly. Some churches are growing here and there all across the United States.

At Home

In the North Arkansas Conference, we had a net loss in membership for sixteen years. Because I was sounding off nationally, people asked me what I was doing at home. Well, we've been working at it. We finally turned our losses around, but just barely. A net gain of twenty-one souls in 1987 required a Herculean effort by hundreds of churches.

According to the leadership of the conference, these factors caused the North Arkansas turnaround: the establishment of new congregations, emphasis on the Sunday school, promoting pastors who make disciples, and the Five Star Plan. The Five Star Plan highlights simple spiritual thrusts that every congregation ought to be making anyway. It emphasizes growth values. An appreciation breakfast each year gives affirmation to churches that succeed.

We started simply, giving five clear goals.

*Increase Sunday school attendance by 5 percent
*Start one new Sunday school class
*Receive 1 person by profession of faith for every 75 members
*Conduct a membership training class
*Pay all missionary and conference apportionments.

Modest? Yes, but still it lifted up a set of values and provided a challenge.

Four years later we're more flexible, giving more initiative to the local church. I wrote to each pastor and each lay member for suggestions in building the new Five Star Plan. Some tiny churches can't start a new class each year. Some large churches have trouble meeting the profession of faith goals, although the largest church in our denomination, First United Methodist Church in Houston, leads the way each year in persons received by profession of faith.

So, thanks to their suggestions, the latest Five Star Plan has been established (see page 27).

It's elementary as ABC. But it is amazing how many pastors are not equipped to accomplish these primary tasks. Far too few church men and women are able to do the basic job of making disciples.

With so much of Arkansas in a rural population decline, the slight growth is an exhilarating victory. It shows that most conferences can grow if they want to. When the lay members and pastors of "five star" churches gather for a recognition breakfast at Annual Conference, happy testimonies interrupt each other. Time never is adequate to hear all the signs and wonders of growing churches.

The United Methodist Church

Arkansas Area . . . Richard B. Wilke, *Bishop*

The Five Star "Plan of Excellence"

—A Challenge For Every Church

1989

★ 1. MEMBERSHIP:

a. Pastoral contact with each family.
b. Lay call on every constituent.
c. Receive one new member on profession of faith or reaffirmation for each 100 members.
d. Conduct a confirmation class using approved confirmation materials.

★ 2. SUNDAY SCHOOL: (Three out of the four following:)

a. Start a new Sunday School Class.
b. Have Sunday School members call on inactive/constituency members before Rally Day in the Fall.
c. Have a 5% increase in Sunday School Attendance.
d. Have ½ of the Sunday School teachers in a training event during the year.

★ 3. FINANCE: (Four out of five of the following:)

a. Have a tithing emphasis.
b. Pay apportionments in full for the year.
c. Participate in the Hunger Ingathering.
d. Support an Advance Special.
e. Meet the "Catch The Vision" Goal (1 in 20 members) in the NAC; Complete the New Church Development "Fairshare" in LRC.

★ 4. YOUTH MINISTRIES:

a. Send one youth to camp or district or conference rally.
b. Start a "new" youth ministry (Scout troop, youth choir, UMY, Sunday School class, etc.).

★ 5. CREATIVE MINISTRIES:

Develop one new, self initiated, program for the Church. May be evangelism, community service, ministry with singles, etc., etc.

As each goal is completed, contact the District Superintendent for the seal to affirm the completion.

Churches achieving these goals will be recognized at Annual Conference.

Contributions from Abroad

The missionary enterprise is bearing fruit, some thirtyfold, some sixtyfold, some one hundredfold. We should celebrate the dramatic results of the missionary movement. Today, in many parts of the world, the Christian church burns like a forest fire. Now, with their enthusiasm, our spiritual children are models to inspire us and have much to teach us.

Let me use Africa as an example, although Korea, Latin America, and the Philippines could be used as well.

Mozambique

I interviewed Mary Jean Tennent and Bishop Joao Somane Machado of Mozambique. Miss Tennent, longtime missionary, told me that the Protestant churches stood with the people in their recent struggle for freedom. The early government, receiving aid and counsel from the Soviet Union, cracked down on churches and took over some schools. Yet, the churches, with their hospitals and clinics, continued to care for all people. Now in a freer atmosphere the church rolls are exploding. Native leadership is in place. People remember the blood of the Christian martyrs. Worship—preaching, music, dancing, giving, celebrating—is African, not "Western." Thousands are coming.

Today the government wants to hire Protestant Christians because they are honest, they come to work on time, and they work hard. Mainline denominations trained local leaders. When missionaries were imprisoned or evacuated, the work went on. Missionaries are returning to work alongside African leadership. Two women, even as I write, are training in Portugal, one to be a hospital administrator and trainer, the other a teacher of nursing. Two couples are going as agriculturalists. Missionaries work as brothers and sisters in Christ alongside African leadership. But hundreds more are needed.

Bishop Machado explained: "Oh, Bishop, when you come, you will see that these people, the children, are singing spiritual songs."

"African songs?" I asked him. "The music as well as the words?"

Bishop Machado answered: "Yes, we use tom-toms and xylophones. We use traditional African melodies. When we have the offering, all the people come forward, dancing and singing. The old come; children come. We're clapping, filling the aisles. It is wonderful! With the African music, the language, the culture, the dance—it's no longer an imported church. I think that now we have become African Christianity."

I asked, "How do they reach people not in the church?"

"Oh, it is easy, " he assured me. "The beginning is when you have one friend in some family. When you talk to this friend about becoming a Christian, all the family comes because he will be the preacher in the family now. It's not you. Ten or twenty in this family come because one of them is now a Christian. 'This is the way; this is the church; this is the way to praise God. This is the true God,' he will say to the family. Tomorrow you will see twenty new people who want to become members of this church. Then we will have a class for them."

"How long will you train new converts?" I inquired.

"We do this six months—for new converts. And then we baptize. Then we have other classes for people to become members."

"Are they on probation even after they are baptized?" I asked.

He answered, "Yes. We train probationers another six months before they become full members. They must learn from the Bible what it means to be a Christian."

"Now," I said, "let me ask you this: You are starting new churches. How do you do that?"

"In this evangelization we have some of our members move to the other side of the city. These members start a class there. Then a lay leader goes there to see what they have—ten or twenty. Then the leader will ask a pastor to visit. Then when the congregation becomes big—fifty people—we have a provisional local church—with fifty."

"And then do you use a lay pastor?"

"Yes, we use a lay pastor," he responded, "whom we call a lay preacher. We use lay preachers until there are a hundred full members in the local church. Every church starts new congregations—all the time—many new churches. We are growing all the time."

Angola

Bishop de Carvalho, of Angola, helped me to see the signs and wonders even more clearly. Like other leaders, he was tortured by the Portuguese. Now he serves two annual conferences, 110,000 United Methodist members in 500 congregations. Each church is continually helping to start or sponsor another church.

"We thirst to make the church truly Christian, truly African," he told me. "The cross is the sign of liberation for us, spiritual liberation, the vertical arm; political and social liberation, the horizontal arm. Colonialism by Portugal tried to destroy the churches, but we survived. Now we have undressed the African church from its Western clothes. We will take the good news of liberation to all of Africa."

He explained further, "Some Americans have been paranoid about Africa—afraid it wants to fall into Satan's hands, into communism. We are deeply religious people with powerful community feelings. The Christian churches are working together, helping us both to return to our roots of awe and wonder and to move forward to our freedom in Christ."

I asked about the miracles of the past few years, in a raped and ravaged land. "Leadership, almost nonexistent when the Portuguese left, is emerging. The missionaries helped develop African leadership."

Zaire

Bishop Fama Onema of Zaire described the church in his country. "When I became bishop in 1972, we had 100,000 members and one bishop. In 1976 membership doubled, giving us two bishops and an expansion of primary and secondary schools. Now we have five annual conferences, 400,000 members, and three bishops. The lay leader of the conference is the secretary of education for the government. Other leaders

LIBRARY
BRYAN COLLEGE
DAYTON, TENN. 37321

in government and business and professional people are
graduates of our schools. A few of our pastors are educated, some
with doctorates, but many of them are uneducated. Lay pastors
get up from a town church, walk to a village, and start a new
congregation."

Zimbabwe

Bishop Abel Muzorewa's political influence helped wrench
Zimbabwe (formerly Rhodesia) from British rule. Again, the
churches stood with the people, praying, working for indepen-
dence, and providing clinics and schools. Their institutions are
part and parcel of church life.

"I deliberately appointed four pastors to head our most
important schools," he told me. I warned him that in America
many of our church schools, colleges, and universities have
become secular, lost to the church's witness. He replied, "We
want to learn from that experience. The new United Methodist
University, which the church hopes to build in Zimbabwe, will
begin as a seminary. As it expands in education, social work,
medicine, engineering, and political science, we want it to be
African and Christian."

Four hundred United Methodist churches with 56,000
members are growing at a rate of 5 to 10 percent a year. When I
thought of the political and social turmoil, few roads, refugees
streaming into Zimbabwe, I thought of the impossibilities. The
bishop smiled, "It is a time of unbelievable opportunity for
God," he said.

So there you have it—mainline denominations in the United
States are still in steady decline, but are spotted by congregations
alive and vibrant. Key growth pastors want to help. Some
churches, working in difficult circumstances, minister to people
in their needs—and grow. Whole sections of the church are
shaking themselves and trying to awake from their slumber.

We are surrounded by a great cloud of witnesses, offspring of
the missionary movement in Africa and around the world. Our
eyes should sparkle at the work of God in so many places. It is a
time of New Testament power. The book of Acts could be
written today. Once again, "many signs and wonders [are] done
among the people by the hands of the apostles" (Acts 5:12).

CHAPTER TWO

Rebirthing the Church

Can a church be born again?

Can Presbyterians enter again into the spiritual womb of Calvin? Can Lutherans enter the spiritual womb of Luther? Can Methodist groups in the United States enter again the spiritual womb of Asbury and come out circuit riders?

What about a local congregation? Can a church return to its birthing days? "How can a man be born when he is old?" asked Nicodemus. "Can he enter a second time into his mother's womb?" (John 3:4). Jesus answered him: "That which is born of flesh is flesh. . . . You must be born anew . . . of the Spirit" (John 3:6-8). Can a church be born again, from above?

Organizations Need Renewal

Institutions in America cry out for renewal. They are old and tired. "We are reinventing education, health care, politics, and virtually all our social structures," claim John Naisbitt and Patricia Aburdene in *Re-Inventing the Corporation*. Steel mills have become obsolete; automobile manufacturers ran out of gas; public schools are producing functional illiterates. Organizations either renew or die.

Mainline churches have been sidelined for thirty years. Ten major Protestant denominations that have shown growth continually from colonial times started on the skids in the early 1960s.

Aging and growing rigidity are normal patterns. My tennis game isn't what it used to be—sore elbow and stiff knees and all that. Students of Troeltsch and Richard Neibuhr know that fire-in-the-eye sects start out as movements. Then they adopt by-laws, set up committees, and become churches. They lose momentum.

John W. Gardner explains this pattern in *Self Renewal:* "When organizations and societies are young, they are flexible, fluid, not yet paralyzed by rigid specialization and willing to try anything once. As the organization ages, vitality diminishes, flexibility gives way to rigidity, creativity fades and there is a loss of capacity to meet challenges from unexpected directions."

Institutions, like people, become set in their ways. Patterns become ruts. Habits feel comfortable. Early enthusiasm wanes. John, in Revelation, warned the church at Ephesus, "You have abandoned the love you had at first" (Rev. 2:4). Jesus put it like this: You cannot put new wine in old wineskins.

Is Renewal Possible?

Some institutions have the capacity for renewal. Sometimes an organization can be reborn. But it's as tough as learning to walk again after suffering a stroke. Change is both painful and difficult. Naisbitt and Aburdene, in *Re-Inventing the Corporation,* claim: "It takes from 20 to 40 minutes for a mammoth, ocean-going tanker weighing 300,000 tons to change its course. A big corporation with tens of thousands of employees finds it very difficult to adapt swiftly to sudden changes in the environment."

Renewal, of course, is more than mere change. Reshuffling personnel, renaming the agencies, and rewriting the by-laws may bring change, but not renewal. It is proverbial now to compare such antics to rearranging the deck chairs on the Titanic. Renewal means rebirth, revitalization, and new energy. Renewal means creativity and newly directed energy.

Renewal is not growth for growth's sake. A hospital may

expand and go broke. Much of the "church growth" literature misses the point of spiritual revitalization. New members, unconverted and undisciplined, quickly become dead wood. Some high growth churches add numbers to the roll but not names in the Book of Life. Statistical bloat gives church growth a bad name—after all, cancer is a high growth organism. High growth ought not to be purchased with cheap grace.

But renewal can happen. Trinity Church in downtown Denver, because of inner-city blight, pastoral turmoil, and a disastrous fire, declined between 1956 and 1979. From being one of the leading churches in the conference (nearly 4,000 members), the church declined to being 1,000 members struggling hard for survival. Now, as Lyle Schaller says, it is "the miracle at 18th and Broadway."

Beginning in 1980, the church began to grow. With a new senior pastor—Reverend James Barnes—an aggressive calling program, the formation of new adult classes, the organizing of singles ministries, lots of new choirs, and a strong children's ministry, Old Trinity has grown to 2,000 members. The church pays its apportionments in full each year, and, in cooperation with a major corporation, has rebuilt the entire education building.

Old Trinity, in the heart of the city, is alive and well, reborn to a new future.

What Causes Renewal?

According to some experts, two elements must be present for social change to occur: new values and economic necessity. It takes both. Neither force is powerful enough to produce social change on its own.

For example, in a free economy, a business organization is the quickest and most responsive to change. Customers, unlike political constituents, vote every day, hastening corporate change. One-third of the restaurants and cafes in our country go broke each year. If the steak is tough or the prices too high, the people go elsewhere. They vote with their feet.

Corporations knew about a change in American values during the 1960s. New "people-oriented" value systems stirred the air. But the companies did not try to change until they were hit by the economic necessities of the 1970s. The drop in sales rattled their cages. For some businesses, it was too late; foreign competition had already filled the gap.

Many congregations wait too long to change their ways. Others listen to winds of the Spirit before they hear the dread footsteps of economic necessity.

Old Asbury Church in Little Rock, Arkansas, was located downtown in a neighborhood gone commercial. The city government razed hundreds of homes to make way for the interstate highway. Yet, the people kept up the building and ministered to older members who drove in from all over the city. The young pastor wanted to relocate; the longtime members resisted. A former beloved pastor, since retired, came back and helped interpret the two elements needed for change. First, he reminded parishioners of earlier evangelical values. He pointed to a city filled with children and youth who needed the church the way their own children had needed it years before.

Second, he reminded them that once they had supported missionaries, kept the property attractive, and given help to denominational institutions. Now they couldn't pay their bills. They faced economic crisis.

So a difficult change was made. Asbury relocated. Now their new buildings brim with preschool aged children, youth play in the gym, and adult classes fill the rooms on Sunday. Even the old-timers rejoice in their revitalized church. Asbury does not worship in a permanent sanctuary yet, but they are an alive congregation. In this example, both elements for renewal are present: new values and economic necessity.

Here's another analysis. Tom Peters uses "chaos" as his concept of renewal, calling his book *Thriving on Chaos*. He argues that some confusion is necessary for creativity to occur. Others have spoken of "creative destruction," that painful process by which old structures and techniques are dismantled and renewed by a fresh dynamism. The ultimate question for any system, organization, or institution is whether it is rigid, impervious to change, or whether a built-in suppleness allows it to adapt to new challenges.

In the churches, we do everything possible to avoid confusion and to maintain control. Too much control, however, locks out new ideas. When we read the account of the chaos in the church in Corinth, we understand Tom Peter's thesis. Chaos was the context for conversions in Corinth. Drunkenness at Holy Communion, sexual promiscuity, worshipers speaking in unknown tongues—a wild bunch, those Corinthians. In the midst of such chaotic conditions, God gave birth to a new church. The new Corinthian church led people of all walks of life to Jesus. They burned with such spiritual intensity that they became Paul's "letter of recommendation" (II Cor. 3:2).

Today we have more order—and less power. So little is out of control that scarcely any room remains for creativity. The danger in our denominations is creeping inflexibility, what might be called church sclerosis, the loss of the ability to change and adapt. For renewal to come, people must have space for new ideas, and that requires flexible structures. Entrepreneurs need some freedom to invent new forms of ministry.

Order is not our problem. Running out of steam is. The systems are not breaking down; they are running down. Leaders attend church meetings, but too few conversions occur. The organization has become so tightly structured that it takes all our energies to maintain it. New energy must be brought into the system.

For example, consider Metropolitan United Methodist Church in Detroit, Michigan. It was running down like a clock until energized by new spiritual vitality.

I asked my friend William K. Quick, pastor of Metropolitan Church, why he used radio in his ministry. It's hard work, recording weekly on two stations.

Quick laughed, "My face is better suited for radio than for T.V. Besides, thousands of people, tens of thousands, listen to the church's message on radio."

When I came to Metropolitan Church fifteen years ago, I realized that the stately old church once had thousands in worship, but now had dropped to 250 that summer. In that huge city we needed visibility. I needed to communicate with a lot of people fast. I was asked by WJR, "the Great Voice of the Great Lakes," to provide, once a month, 75 seconds of "Point of View."

In a human interest news clip format, I always sought to put in a good word for Jesus. We also broadcast "City Pulpit" on WEXL, Royal Oak, Michigan, for five minutes right before the 6:00 P.M. news, during "drive out time" for Detroiters. We also broadcast on WJR a twenty-five minute sermon and music on Sunday.

I could not have taken the message of the church to the throngs of the city more quickly. Nothing else would have given Metropolitan more visibility. Now 800 or more worshipers attend on Sunday, and Metropolitan has a voice to the city.

Bill concluded, "Please remind pastors in small towns and country villages that the local radio station can be a powerful ally in ministry. I did it in Zebulon, North Carolina, long before I came to Detroit." His ministry includes much more, but his radio programs put the "zap" in a big old downtown church. Maxie Dunnam has done the same thing with Christ Church in Memphis.

Leadership

Whenever people discuss renewal, they usually begin by mentioning leadership. Lee Iacocca turned Chrysler around. Lou Holtz took the Notre Dame football team to a national championship. Pastor-parish or pulpit committees today often ask for a "leader."

Many business and church leaders were trained as managers or counselors. Now we need a new breed. "Successful C.E.O.'s must see themselves as leaders, not managers" (Naisbitt and Aburdene, *Re-Inventing the Corporation*). I once received sound advice from the chair of my pastor-parish committee. I had just published a book on marriage group counseling after considerable special training. He said, "No extended counseling. We need a pastor, a preacher, a leader for the *whole* congregation, not just counselors for a few. Refer your extended counseling to someone else." He pointed me in the right direction.

Today's pastor helps a body of believers move forward in faith and ministry. That requires leadership.

John W. Gardner, Jr., in *Leadership Papers*, carefully

defines leadership as "the process of persuasion and example by
which an individual (or leadership team) induces a group to take
action that is in accord with the leaders' purposes or the shared
purposes of all."

Gardner expands his definition of leadership by focusing on
the tasks of a leader.

Envision goals. Today's leaders must be increasingly vision-
ary. Walter O'Brian, president of Hanover Insurance, calls
them "mental pictures." A leader sees what his or her church
could be, could do. "Where there is no vision, the people
perish" (Prov. 29:18 KJV).

Affirm values. Values decay "out there" unless they are
freshly underlined. Tithing leaders develop tithing congregations. A pastor who neglects to pay merchants or who is sexually
undisciplined models defeat for a congregation. Congregations
need and expect personal integrity. A church that exhibits
compassion for the outcast, justice for all people, and forgiveness for the sinsick affirms historic apostolic values and attracts
newcomers.

Motivate. Positive-minded leaders are continually inspiring
their people. A pastor of a small, struggling congregation told
me that he and his wife gave $100 extra at Christmas for world
service apportionments and asked the congregation to do the
same. The next Sunday, $5,000 was received. That's motiva-
tional leadership. Everybody celebrated.

Manage. After putting it down, now we lift it up. Keeping the
process purring is necessary. Wise pastors empower laity,
secretaries, or staff to do most of it—which is actually a style of
top management. Laypersons with gifts of administration can
sometimes shore up pastors who have weak management skills,
if the pastors will let them.

Unify. Most pastors and church leaders fail because "they
can't work with people." A key ingredient for leaders is the
ability to hear. Woodrow Wilson wrote, "The ear of the leader
must ring with the voices of the people." Leaders who listen
well draw people together.

Interpret. Leaders constantly communicate values, continually reaffirm directions, always remind people of who they are
and what they are called to do.

Model. You don't like this one, do you? Especially preachers. Who wants to be a "goody two shoes?" But who said that was the image we want to convey? Church leaders who call on lost souls, take lonely kids or unwed mothers into their homes, are symbols, too. Strong Christian couples who have adopted children who have physical handicaps or from racially mixed backgrounds make a powerful statement.

Innovate. The old paths are often blocked. Old solutions no longer solve anything. Our times call for "transformational leadership." Systemic stagnation requires a redesign of strategy. If we are burying more people than we are baptizing, we must not be doing something right.

Dwight D. Eisenhower, so gifted in leading complex organizations, put it in a nutshell when he said, "I'll tell you what leadership is: It's persuasion . . . and conciliation . . . and education . . . and patience."

Leaders with a Vision

The church was born on Pentecost with an explosion of kingdom vision. Peter, filled with the Holy Spirit, called out:

> This is what was spoken by the prophet Joel: . . .
> I will pour out my Spirit upon
>   all flesh,
> and your sons and your daughters
>   shall prophesy,
> and your young men shall see
>   visions,
> and your old men shall dream
>   dreams.
> (Acts 2:16-17)

That pentecostal vision became the apostolic message: "Jesus of Nazareth, a man attested to you by God with mighty works and wonders and signs . . . this Jesus . . . you crucified" (Acts 2:22, 23). This Jesus God raised up, and of that we are all witnesses. "Being therefore exalted at the right hand of God, and having received from the Father the promise of the Holy Spirit, he has poured out this which you see and hear. . . .

Repent, and be baptized, every one of you . . . for the forgiveness of your sins; and you shall receive the gift of the Holy Spirit"
(Acts 2:33, 38). The apostles never lost sight of the central gospel.

The apostles never let the gospel vision escape them. When
the widows argued about food, preachers were tempted to be
distracted, but they said, "It is not right for us to neglect the
preaching of God's word in order to handle finances" (Acts 6:2
GNB). "We ourselves, then, will give our full time to prayer
and the work of preaching" (Acts 6:4 GNB).

Does your congregation have a vision? I wish every church
would draw an invisible circle around the church, twenty
minutes by car in every direction, and dream of offering grace
and the fellowship of Jesus Christ to everyone in that radius.

We asked a young preacher and spouse to start new work in an
old downtown church building in the historic quarter of the city.
A core of 40 laypeople agreed to help. Last month they made
20,000 telephone calls to everyone in the phone book—young,
old, black, white, rich, poor. They invited them to "come and
see." It was a vision, mystical and practical. Ninety visitors came
in the snow—a victory for a new congregation in a great old
church. I used to say to the Christian Church (Disciples of
Christ), the American Baptists, the Presbyterians, and the
United Methodists, that it takes a while to turn the ship around,
having in my mind the Queen Elizabeth II changing course. Now
I see it more as a flotilla of ships, needing to change course. After
all we have no pope, no C.E.O. who can ramrod change. Maybe
renewal will come from thousands of local church leaders who are
recaptured by a vision of a world reborn in Christ Jesus. Maybe
you are one of the leaders we're looking for.

Women in Leadership

One source of new creativity is the women leaders who are
emerging at all levels of the church. Women and men in
witness, service, ministry, and governance are walking arm in
arm together. The Chinese say that "women hold up half the
sky." The church of the future will be lifted up by gifted leaders
of both sexes.

Some people misunderstand I Corinthians 14:34 and try to use it today to hold women back. When they read, "The women should keep silent in the churches," they don't understand what was happening in the Corinthian church. The Holy Spirit had put women right in the heart of the fellowship. Women, new converts without Jewish training or social upbringing, were carried away with zeal. The church at Corinth gave them new freedom. In their joy and exuberance, they let their hair down like women of the streets. They asked questions and talked too much. Paul gave pastoral advice to try to restore some order. He said, in effect, that they should behave in a dignified manner, show some decorum. They should respect the customs and ask their husbands questions when they get home. "Be subordinate, even as the [civil and Jewish] law says" (I Cor. 14:34). Paul was trying to keep the revolution from blowing the tub out of the water.

But Paul was filled with Jesus' spirit when he shouted a central reality of the revolution: "There is neither male nor female . . . in Christ Jesus" (Gal. 3:28). The Holy Spirit was at work, and the social customs would change.

If we are to rebirth the church, we need women in leadership. They must not keep silent. We need to use all of our resources. We need women, as well as men, as pastors, teachers, administrators, superintendents, and bishops. They will bring original ideas, new insight, and fresh enthusiasm.

It is sad when churches are afraid to have women as pastors. All my life I've experienced women in leadership roles. My grandmother, in the family funeral home, was driving a hearse in 1917 and running the business as a widow in 1932. In the family funeral home, my mother made midnight death calls all through the 1930s and 1940s. The finest administrator I have ever known was Mrs. Olive Ann Beech, former president of Beech Aircraft. She often chaired the building campaign or board of trustees. One of the ablest lay leaders I ever had was Margaret Selfridge, widow and bank executive. When she spoke, people listened.

By the year 2000, one-third of the members of the legal profession will be women. One-third of new businesses are now created by women. In many denominational seminaries, over 30 percent of the students are women.

Lee Iacocca bemoans the fact that corporations, needing new imaginative ideas, have been slow to accept women in management. In *Talking Straight*, he says: "There's an area of management where I feel our company and many others have really blown it, and that's women in management. The funny thing is that even though all of us in Detroit have told ourselves that autos are a man's world, we've got plenty of women on the assembly lines in the factories. If it's a man's world, why are the plants so full of women?"

Church groups who look especially to the Holy Spirit—Holiness, Assembly of God, Salvation Army—have known this truth for a long time. Their women ministers have been creative and productive. The understanding is written deep in Scripture. Lydia, Paul's first convert in Philippi, organized the first house church there. Syntyche and Euodia were leaders in the Philippian church. "To each is given the manifestation of the Spirit for the common good" (I Cor. 12:7). "Having gifts that differ according to the grace given us, let us use them" (Rom. 12:6).

Will women in pastoral ministry create problems in the church? You bet. The itinerancy system will twist and bend. Women ministers married to farmers can only go so far from home. Combining two careers is tough, sometimes too tough. Marriage and babies and pastoral ministry may be too much for both husband and wife. Even careers less stressful than pastorates are difficult. "The price is very high," said the mother of a two-year-old daughter and a partner of a prestigious law firm. "The emotional turmoil, the exhaustion, the frustration of having too many things to do and not enough time."

So what should the church do? Bend the system. Give people time for rest, for care of children with husbands or wives taking leave, part-time pastorates, forms of ministries other than pressure packed pastorates. Don't worry so much about prestige and salary. Look for forms of respite. Emphasize comraderie more and competition less.

God has gifted women by his Spirit. We cannot deny the Holy Spirit.

Structural Changes

Grass Roots

Renewal is complex. Even if we have strong spiritual leaders, they must have a strategy. How do we go about rebuilding an institution like the church? Let's look at ways renewal comes about, using examples from church and business. In particular, I want to highlight three approaches: grass roots initiative, networking, and decentralization.

"Despite the conceits of New York and Washington, almost nothing starts there. America is a bottom up society. New trends and ideas begin in cities and local communities. Trends are generated from the bottom up" (John Naisbitt, *Megatrends*). Renewal starts with individuals who have new ideas, usually at the local level.

Sounds just like the Acts of the Apostles, doesn't it? Rome, the capital of the empire, was the last stop on Paul's missionary travels, not the first. Athens, the cultural center of the empire, was too sophisticated to appropriate the salvation message. New life began for people in the villages of Samaria, nondescript cities like Antioch, and rough, melting pot ports like Corinth.

Too many pastors and too many churches are waiting for a program from "on high"—not from God, mind you, but from "somewhere up there." As Russell Conwell observed long ago, the diamonds are usually right in our own backyards.

Most new businesses start small, not in large corporate headquarters, but in garages, basements, or storefronts. Most creative ministries are inspired by the Holy Spirit and innovated into existence by local churches.

If your church is like the paralyzed man waiting beside the pool of Bethesda for someone to put it in the water, don't be surprised if you wait for thirty-eight years. Who knows the territory better than you? Who knows the needs in the local area better than the policemen, the school teachers, the social workers, the doctors, the court judges, the Salvation Army, and the pastors right there in the town where you live?

Psychologists use the term *learned helplessness*. Children

whose parents do everything for them or spouses who "lean" all the time exhibit this learned behavior pattern. Some churches are like that. They wait for a $500 grant from headquarters before building a wheelchair ramp. They expect the denominational magazine to mandate their mission.

Woodlawn United Methodist Church in Derby, Kansas, had plateaued. Located in a highly mobile community, the church wanted more fellowship. The Sunday school needed strengthening. They required a wider, more informal port of entry. One man said, "Why don't we men fix breakfast for everybody each Sunday morning?" Now stoves are turned on at 6:30 A.M. A rotating crew of ten men (men only) prepare eggs, bacon, biscuits, juice, and coffee each Sunday from 7:30 until 9:30 A.M. Sixty men are on the schedule. Attendance at early church is up. Sunday school attendance is up. Visitors bring other visitors to breakfast. One hundred fifty or more people eat together on Sunday morning. Local idea, local work, self-initiated—successful.

Top executives always know where the action is. Lee Iacocca says, "Never forget, the assembly line makes the money. The staff doesn't make a dime." The local church makes the converts, trains the disciples, counsels the troubled, and buries the dead.

We used to think missions were done far away by someone else. Without undermining missionaries (we need more, lots more) or destroying coordinating staff (who need to be closer to the people), we now put the spotlight right where it belongs, right on the local congregation. "Mission" is what your church does in your town. When you read the New Testament, you read what God did in the church in Ephesus, in Philippi, in Antioch, in Jerusalem, in Galatia, and in the towns and cities of Samaria. Christian travelers were witnesses, evangelists, or teachers. They moved because of economic or political pressure, or they were driven by spiritual motivation. They gave encouragement to the local churches or helped start new ones.

Networking

Networking is a "buzz" word. Management consultants use it and get paid $1,000 a day. Networking is an ingredient for renewal. Christians have understood networking for twenty centuries. In the book of Acts, travelers share their salvation experiences in homes and synagogues. The signs and wonders of healings, conversions, and bold testimonies served as supper table conversation for the saints. Watch Paul make tents with Aquila and Priscilla in Corinth in Acts 18. Each Sabbath they argued in the synagogue, persuading Jews and Greeks. Silas and Timothy dropped in from Macedonia and swapped stories. Paul took his tentmaker friends with him to several towns, then to Ephesus. A preacher named Apollos was testifying there, but he didn't have the story right. Aquila and Priscilla straightened him out so that he was able to show "by the scriptures that the Christ was Jesus" (Acts 18:28).

Notice the interweaving of relationships in II Timothy. Paul, in prison in Rome, has "finished the race" (II Tim. 4:6). He says:

> Luke alone is with me. Get Mark . . . for he is very useful. . . . Tychicus I have sent to Ephesus. When you come, bring the cloak . . . also the books, and above all the parchments. . . . Greet [Priscilla] and Aquila, and the household of Onesiphorus. . . . Do your best to come before winter.
> (II Timothy 4:11-21)

Networking is an ingredient for renewal.

Most of the New Testament is correspondence racing back and forth within the movement, giving counsel, insight, and encouragement. The information flow was horizontal, not vertical.

With the development of huge organizations with layers of administrative structures, leadership now struggles with communications "up and down" the system. In church structures, national boards and agencies wonder why pastors won't read their mimeographed mail or the official magazines. Pastors and key laity wonder why bishops, general secretaries, and denominational executives don't pay attention to things happening in local congregations. General Halftrack at base camp in the "Beetle Bailey" comic strip keeps waiting for a message from the Pentagon, but the letter never comes.

American industry, bogged down with fifty years of vertical structures, is breaking loose. "The U. S. industrial economy, tailor-made for hierarchical structures, fell into deep trouble. Rising up in its place was the new informational economy where hierarchies were badly out of time" (Naisbitt, *Megatrends*). People have been forced to talk to one another, sharing ideas, information, and resources.

We ought not to be too critical of our church superstructures; they served us in the past. We need to redesign them for a new day. The people are good people, doing their jobs. The system worked well when missionaries traveled by steamship and books took three years to publish. It worked well when a rural church in Ohio was not too much different from a rural church in Oregon and both needed help to fulfill their mission. But now local needs vary, communication is fast, and travel is easy. Now leadership gets people together locally who can solve their own problems.

Ministers of three-point charges know better how to help one another than anybody else. Covenant groups, sharing fellowships, breakfast gatherings all across the country help folks to share ideas with one another.

Networking is occurring in youth ministries. Workers with youth are surely the loneliest leaders in the church. The burn out rate is two years for full-time people. They experience little support—from parents of the youth, conferences, or denominations. When many major denominations abandoned youth ministries in the early 1960s (after some brilliant work in the 1940s and 1950s), youth ministers were left high and dry. Today many conferences have no staff help in youth ministries. So what is happening? Youth workers flock to conferences sponsored by independent Christian youth organizations. They are starved for information and fellowship; they run to any source of help. Newsletters spring up informally with hundreds of youth directors sharing with one another—networking.

While the denomination argues over the structure of youth ministries in the denominational hierarchy, workers with youth are trying to help one another make Christ real to kids.

Decentralization

"Centralized structures are crumbling all across America, but our society is not falling apart. Far from it. The people of this country are rebuilding America from the bottom up. . . . We are moving from centralization to decentralization" (Naisbitt, *Megatrends*).

I love the connectional nature of my denomination. But our connectional church once had room for personal relationships. In the 1950s, we knew missionaries by name and helped support them. Now local churches are struggling to pay "apportionments" with little zeal and few dollars left for extra-mile giving. At the same time that the people are demanding a face-to-face relationship, the organization has become increasingly "far away." Willimon and Wilson agree: "The organization has become a handicap to the creation of a vital church. It is ironic that at a time in which the educational level of the clergy, and probably that of the laity, has never been higher, the patronizing instructions given to the local church concerning how they should be organized and what they should do have also reached an all time high."

Walk into strong mission-minded—perhaps "independent"—church and see the map on the wall. A string is tied from their church to the picture of a missionary doctor in Angola, an evangelist in Costa Rica, a physical therapist in India, a teacher in Hong Kong. Pinned nearby is a monthly newsletter from one of "their" missionaries. Home on furlough, the missionaries teach in the Sunday school and preach from the pulpit. They are known and loved by the congregation. Weaknesses exist in this system, of course. Some missionaries receive strong support, others soft. Some missionaries' strategies lack ongoing continuity. I don't want to lose interrelatedness. We can do some glorious things together, such as building a university in Africa. I'm glad that our missionaries do not have to spend much of their time raising money, like those independent churches I mentioned. But we have almost lost the personal touch. We need to reclaim the relationship with the local church.

A Presbyterian pastor knew he could strengthen the spiritual life of his congregation if he could interest them in missions. He took a work team to Presbyterian missions in Central America. They developed personal relationships and exchanged communications. A great earthquake ravaged the churches, the mission station, and the homes of the people, so the congregation raised $100,000 in medicine, blankets, and emergency supplies and took it by plane to approved points of need. They were severely reprimanded by their national headquarters for not going through official channels, even though they touched every official base and worked only with Presbyterian personnel. The pastor and the parishioners were so angry by this action that they have broken all financial ties with the denomination. Why? They want a piece of the action. They now are doing three times as much for missions as before.

The United Methodist Women plead for members to send money to "undesignated giving." In theory, that allows money to be placed appropriately by those few in authority who understand the situation. But in practice, only a few feel the excitement of knowing where the money is going. All but the hard core drift to other interests. The money begins to dry up because people don't feel any relationship. People give money to people, not to systems. It is only human to want to feel a part of a specific ministry.

Some men and women—United Methodists, Presbyterians, Baptists—from Augusta, Arkansas, have been drilling water wells in Haiti for several years. They have bought their own equipment, paid their own travel expenses, communicated with local church and government authorities, and informed denominational boards of missions of what they are doing. They have steadily drilled, equipped, and trained maintenance people for over ninety wells, providing good water for thousands of people. They never have to beg for money. People want to help. It is the spirit of decentralization. It is the spirit of our times.

Superintendents crack the whip to make certain that all apportionments are paid. It is becoming increasingly difficult because even they can't remember what all the money goes for. Connectional askings are necessary, of course, but the local church must also have a personal, hands on relationship with missionary projects. Lower the amount of connectional askings and lift up the missional options for a church in renewal.

Consider your congregation's work with young people. If your church wanted to strengthen its ministry to youth, what would you do first? Ask a nearby church? Write a letter to the bishop? Send a delegation to the seminary? Telephone the superintendent? Write a letter to the Department of Youth Ministries? Telephone the Conference office? All or none of the above?

My guess is that you would use the telephone and call an individual you know personally who has special knowledge about youth ministries. So, if a denomination wants to try to convert the teenagers of America to Jesus Christ during the next decade, we need knowledgeable people scattered throughout the country who are visible and accessible. Do we have them? Sure. There are hundreds of magnificent full-time workers throughout the nation. But they are neither visible nor accessible. They are not in the structure, but they could be if the organization were decentralized.

Or take the task of establishing new congregations. The National Division of the General Board of Global Ministries prepared a brochure announcing 200 new churches a year with plans to raise $20 million dollars. The idea collapsed under its own weight. We can't raise money in Arkansas to start a church in Texas, even if our own children have moved there—especially if Arkansas has to send the money first to New York, and Texas has to apply for a grant to receive it!

That's not the way growing denominations do it. First, there has to be a clean structure: a board of church extension whose single job is to help start new Sunday schools and churches and relocate others, with a boss who is held accountable. But then, the leadership must work closely with local groups. The real power is in the districts, the cities, the church cluster.

The leaders in the Southern Baptist Convention and the Assemblies of God take it close to the people. Experts in demographics start work right where they live. They mobilize committed lay community planners, architects, and financial wizards. They inspire and work with pastors and local churches to "mother" new congregations. In short, they decentralize.

If form follows function and if our declining denominations have been asleep like Rip Van Winkle, then let's redesign our structures to get the job done. Let's mobilize new methods close to the people and get going.

> New occasions teach new duties;
> Time makes ancient good uncouth;
> They must upward still, and onward,
> Who would keep abreast of Truth
>   (from "The Present Crisis"
>   by James Russell Lowell)

Mission Driven

Something is still missing. A key piece in the church renewal puzzle has not yet fallen into place. Leadership, of course, is essential—leadership with a vision. Organizations today renew from the ground up, networking and decentralizing. But something is lacking.

To find it, we must look either in the New Testament or at the heart of every vibrant growing congregation. It is clearly in both places. The key ingredient for renewal of the church is mission.

Some businesses claim to be "consumer driven." They listen carefully to each nuance of the public's wishes, trying to respond helpfully and profitably. It makes for a fast-moving, flexible, constantly renewed organization. Another term used in the secular world is *demand,* or *market driven.*

But the church is not a business. Its ministry is more complex than that of a corporation. True, we are, on one hand, driven by the needs of people, similar to an industry's discerning the market. When people are sick or lonely or guilt ridden or afraid, the church is drawn to them as if by a magnetic pull. We are born again whenever we hear the painful cry of the world.

Yet, the mission is not determined by perceived need alone. Market driven, even spiritual, does not explain our compulsive thrust. The world, even in its brokenness, does not set the agenda for the church. Rather, our mission is motivated by the Lord of the church. Jesus Christ gives the commands. His sacred heart pumps blood into the arteries of our ministries.

Christians in the New Testament were mission driven. Look carefully at the early training program. Jesus sent out the seventy, two-by-two. They were not yet strong enough to go one-by-one, as they would later. "Whatever house you enter, first say, 'Peace be to this house. . . .' Eat what is set before you; heal the sick in it and say to them, 'The kingdom of God has come near to you' " (Luke 10:5, 8-9). That Word, incorporated by the church, will bring renewal.

Here's a challenge for churches in small towns: call two-by-two on behalf of the church in every home in the community, giving blessing and asking if the church can be of help. Don't forget the apartment above the hardware store or the trailer house behind the filling station. Larger towns? If your church doesn't have a Fisherman's Club, a witness group, or a weekly telephoning team, you have to ask "Why not?"

The Mormons do not convert people because of their secret golden tablets. They grow because of their two-by-two house calls.

Are you familiar with P.I.E.—Personal Invitational Evangelism? Christian laypersons take a pie, or a loaf of homemade bread, or a plate of cookies to newcomers to their towns, even in huge cities. The effect is overwhelming. "Come in and eat a bite. Who did you say you are? I can't believe anyone would do that in a place this big."

Here's the testimony of one P.I.E. man, an airplane mechanic in Wichita, Kansas.

> "Pieing" people who visit First Church is always enjoyable. Looks of confusion, shock, acceptance and joy, with words of thanks and appreciation, make my role as a pie delivery person (PDP) one I hope to continue doing.
>
> Little known advantages of a PDP are: 1) Picking up the pie(s) on a mid-week afternoon gives me a chance to chat with staff persons without the Sunday hubub; 2) By delivering pies, I explore nooks and crannies of the metro areas and enjoy the clever ways Wichita has for numbering things; and 3) Delivering these tasty treats makes me feel I have a direct hand in doing something, and besides, it's easy.

Sometimes a delivery is just a "thank you for visiting" and expressing a hope that we will see them again in the near future. Other times, pie deliveries are a time to listen and share the Christian walk experiences.

Nine years ago I walked in the front doors of this church, not knowing anyone—no friends, relatives or co-workers. This congregation accepted me, gave me love and helped me grow as a Christian.

By touching another person at just the right time, maybe they also can be as blessed as I feel. We extend the sweetness of a pie; the Lord extends the sweetness of eternal life. Secure in this knowledge and love . . . Dan Hoch.

All sorts of sicknesses become visible—hearts broken by divorce and death, teenagers at loose ends, people without medicine or food or who are alone and depressed. Name the name of Jesus and speak kindly. Some homes will throw you out. "Shake the dust from your feet," said Jesus. Others will experience healing and friendship, first steps toward faith and fellowship. Even the demons are subject to us in the name of the Lord. The four demons of guilt, anxiety, fear, and loneliness can be driven away by the caring concern of gentle Christians.

Mission driven churches are continually praying for ways to serve. In worship services, I hear innumerable pastoral prayers for people dying of cancer. Those are good, but why are there so few prayers for people dying of sin?

Families in our country are being ripped apart like a wounded deer by hungry wolves. Marriages are being ripped asunder. Children are bewildered and confused. What a mission field for the church!

Some congregations, sensing the need and being faithful to Christ, are finding ways to help. Mission driven churches encourage couples to attend "celebrating marriage" or "marriage encounter" weekend retreats while their marriages are still healthy. They put a part-time family counselor on their staff. Study classes on how to have healthy families pop up periodically in their programs. They organize a Christian preschool, a day care center, or a Mom's Day Out to help.

Others try to heal troubled marriages, trying to bring the healing balm of Christ.

A program called "Recovery of Hope" is springing up in church-related hospitals and clinics. Tearing a page or two out of the Alcoholics Anonymous approach, using highly trained therapists, "Recovery of Hope" is changing the structure of many troubled marriages.

Two features are unusually dramatic. A fresh "intensive care" approach provides the couple one week of total immersion in therapy, bringing the full range of testing, counseling, group care and Christian nurture to bear. The success rate, compared to long-term, weekly counseling, is getting high marks.

The second feature affects the ministers and their families. "Clergy Care," a special division of "Recovery of Hope," helps pastors and their spouses through one week of intense evaluation and therapy. Issues like burn out, stress, marital deterioration, chemical abuse, emotional illness, depression, and professional confusion are analyzed and treated. "Recovery of Hope" is the church in mission.

Now focus for a moment on youth. Mission driven churches don't talk about "our youth." They look for every teenager in their town and develop a strategy to help them reach those kids.

AIDS, pre-marital sex, unwed pregnancy, drugs, school drop outs—that's the stuff morning TV talk shows are made of. But we're looking for churches that care enough to open their doors for youth parties after the school football games. We're pleading for churches to enlist or to hire young adults as youth workers to organize work camps, ski trips, singing fellowships, and prayer and study groups. Why do we have only a few kids in our summer youth camps? We could increase these ministries by ten fold if we cared enough.

Some local churches put more money in carpet than they do in kids!

I heard from Kelley Williams from Chapelwood United Methodist Church in Houston. Kelley asks the college students attending his church who are strong Christians to come home in the summer, take regular jobs, and work with the program of the church, particularly with the children and youth. He uses one hundred college students each summer.

In Wichita, we used the same idea, but scaled the number down to twelve students, often slipping to eight or ten. It was revolutionary. We had training weekends for the college students at spring break or as soon as school was out. We paid them $100 for the summer. The young teenagers loved them. Several of the college students later entered full-time youth ministries and other forms of Christian service. Many a small church could do the same thing with one or two students and transform their summer youth programs.

Imagine how thrilled I was to receive a letter from Reverend Richard Wills at Christ Church in Fort Lauderdale, Florida. He wrote: "I thought you would be interested to know that I have picked up your idea concerning the use of college students during the summer as interns. I have talked with one of my laymen and he has agreed to fund the summer project as well as provide the kickoff retreat in the Bahamas, including transportation, for the ten to fifteen college students. I believe this will be a real boost to our church during the summer months."

The "network" is humming. Of course, the youth emphasis is only the beginning, only an example of churches in mission. Concerned congregations will target other areas of population as well. But renewal requires that a church try to fulfill the demands of the gospel.

If you are trying to revitalize the church, at any level, ask what your church is actually doing to transform the lives of people. Under the counsel of Jesus, are you seeing unchurched people in their homes, praying for the sick, offering blessings and casting out demons, inviting people to "come and see"? Churches that are being reborn are mission driven.

So, we return to the question: Can a church be reborn? The answer is a tentative "Yes, if." Is leadership at every level willing to feel the fresh winds of change? Will we be led by the Spirit that gives new visions and dreams? Are we willing to pay the price of change? Where will the new explosions of energy come from? Are we hurting badly enough yet that we cry out for help? Will people at the grass roots burn with new fervor without waiting for a benign nod from headquarters? Will they talk to one another? Can we restructure so that our systems are closer to the people, more accessible to the pain? Can Christians, excited, become a "hands on" priesthood of all believers once again?

A world waits to be saved. Peter going back to his nets can't do it. Only an energized apostolic church can convey the power of God.

I think Christ says continually to his church, "Simon . . . do you love me?" If we will respond like the fisher of men did, "Yes, Lord; you know that I love you," then we will hear the fresh command, "Feed my lambs" (John 21:15).

CHAPTER THREE

Cities That Never Sleep

Climb into your Chevrolet and drive across the great farm-lands of America. Stay off the expressways and toll roads that link major cities. Instead drive the old asphalt two laners, Old 40 or Route 66. Wind your way westward across the gentle hills and valleys of Ohio, through the fertile fields of Indiana and Illinois, into the corn country of Iowa. Gaze at the cattle standing belly deep in the bluegrass of the Kansas Flint Hills. Visit the small towns and the villages that once teemed with children and young people. In your mind's eye, remember farmhouses every quarter or half mile with schoolhouses and open country churches. The land is still productive, but the people are gone.

In the small town, the churches are easy to find. Walk the town square, where you can find the United Methodist church or the Presbyterian church. The Christian church or the Congregational church is just down the street. Red brick, steep steps with columns on the side, a squared off tower of an Akron plan architecture—you can spot it easily. The building itself brings back nostalgic memories of opening exercises in Sunday school with hundreds of people singing "Brighten the Corner Where You Are" or "I Serve a Risen Savior, He's in the World Today."

Stop for Sunday services. Worship with salt of the earth people, most of whom have gray hair. Watch saints with arthritic knees slowly make their way up the steps. Visit the "young adult" class, whose members were born in the 1930s and 1940s. In a quiet, dignified service, worship with faithful, steadfast Christians whose children and grandchildren live in Orange County, California, or in the suburbs of Chicago. Out in the country, the little white frame Disciple or American Baptist churches are gone, not even used for public gatherings or hay barns anymore.

Our Roots Are Rural

A pastor in a church growth seminar asked me, "What would you say differently if you were rewriting *And Are We Yet Alive?*"

I answered that, among other things, I would stress the decline of the rural church. Church renewal literature fails to understand the movement of people and the transformation of values. Oh, we've talked about population movements, the demise of the family farm, and the rapid growth of the cities, but we have not fully stressed the severity of the shift. We have not comprehended the population migration with its unbeliev-able impact on the small town and rural churches. United Methodist churches in Iowa and Kansas lost 5,000 members each last year. Sakes alive, what did we expect! Some say that one quarter of all farmers are United Methodists. No wonder so many of our churches suffer losses.

We have not fully understood the radical emotional and spiritual changes in America. We have not yet envisioned the cities as our turf. We still think and act like citizens of nineteenth-century America.

At the risk of milking a dry cow, let me remind you: When the church's odometer turned "twentieth-century" and main-line Protestant churches were strong in the towns and vibrant in the country, nine families in ten lived on the farm. The Methodist circuit riders had done their work. The Baptist farmer preachers and the Calvinist resident pastors established their congregations across the land. But by the mid 1980s less than three in a hundred persons lived on the land. The picture darkens.

According to Department of Agriculture figures, a farm went out of business every ten minutes in 1985. In 1986, the rate rose to one every seven minutes. Some estimate that by the end of this century at least 200,000 more farmers will have thrown in the towel. Other guesses run as high as a million.

Some folks bemoan the facts. They wring their hands. They remember the smell of new mown alfalfa while they drive their Honda Civics on the northwest highway to downtown Dallas. I put myself through school baling hay. I love the farm. But it's a long way between neighbors. If I had my way, things wouldn't be the way they are. I wish we could airlift millions of people out of the cities and put them in small towns. But economic forces are stronger than feelings. The migration of rural people is gushing into gigantic cities all over the world.

Rural Ministries

Do we abandon our rural churches? Not at all. That would be like Esau selling his birthright. So, let's pause a moment before we go to the metropolis. Without losing our resolve to go where the people from the farm now live, we dare not neglect our town and country.

In fact, we could do a much better job with rural and small town churches than we are doing. Pastors change churches too often. June Hart, a former Peace Corps worker in Brazil, tells about her church in Winona, Missouri—part of a three-point charge. She writes: "When my husband and I came to this community 12 years ago we joined the local United Methodist Church. Since then, there have been nine pastors. That's right, nine pastors in 12 years." She compares the parishioners to the back country people of Brazil, who say, "We aren't even people."

As one who is responsible for making ministerial appointments in an agricultural state, I know how pressure builds to give Reverend Smith a $1,000 raise with a move. Also, some ministers and some spouses are culturally unsuited to the country—can't stand the quiet. But if the itinerant system is, as

Mrs. Hart charges, just like the corporate ladder, with the rural church on the bottom rung, we are adding insult to injury. Instead of giving strength, we are giving weakness. When the school closes, when the old red brick stores on Main Street are boarded up, the old-timers grieve as if their children had died, as if they walked through the cemetery every day. A faithful, caring pastor can provide God's courage and comfort.

One grandmother from a little declining town in the agricultural delta of Arkansas bragged about her pastor: "We have the most wonderful pastor. I just hope you will leave him here forever. He loves us. He comes to see us, and we sit down and visit. He's a fine pastor. He's the first minister we've had in a long time who is not trying to take us somewhere or go somewhere else himself."

Pastors need and use special skills in rural work, just as they require special skills in the city. Saint Paul School of Theology in Kansas City is establishing a chair in Rural Pastoral Ministry. Sounds good. Bishop Reuben Job has appointed a "missioner for church and community development" in rural Iowa. Should be helpful.

Missouri, Kansas, Nebraska, and Arkansas have pioneered in cooperative parish ministries. Half a dozen or so churches can work together to strengthen their spiritual power. If they're not too proud to cooperate with one another, they can have a combined youth ministry, ecumenical services on special occasions, a radio ministry, a men's fellowship, and even special staff workers, like Christian educators or church and community missionaries. Some parishes are ecumenical; some are interracial. Some vibrate with life, even in tiny communities. But some rural churches have a dying mentality, a defensive posture, that works against cooperation or compromise.

In defense of the pastors, I will say that many would be happy to serve in rural communities if the economic base were adequate to support their families. The Arkansas conferences, with one out of seven churches having less than 25 members, have recruited over 400 lay speakers to serve the small churches. One district has added several hundred worship services a year. Our ministries can be improved.

One thing to watch out for is that in many small towns,

"hidden" people live and work. Farm owners are disappearing, bankers and shopkeepers are few, but the little people are there. Keep an eye open for the waitress who slings blue plate specials in the cafe, the two men who work at the grain elevator, the family who lives in a cabin on the edge of town. Some churches say "Nobody lives here anymore," but they forget to count the poor, day laborers, newcomers, and ethnic minorities. Sometimes the Assemblies of God or the Church of Christ will come into that same little community and establish a growing church.

There are a retired preacher and two young fellows just out of college whom I can send to any country church anywhere, and they'll be baptizing folks within three months. They just start calling on every man, woman, child, dog, or cat. Then they talk about Jesus and what it means to become a Christian. Many rural communities are 40 to 50 percent unchurched. Take a look at your county census. You'll be surprised.

Was the Bible Written on the Farm?

Many a preacher waxes eloquent with rural analogies from the Bible. True, the twenty-third Psalm portrays a nomadic pastoral scene with sheep and a shepherd. Jesus spoke of fig trees and lost sheep, of wine skins and fields white unto the harvest.

But the preacher who grew up milking cows, churning butter, or baling hay (or whose father and mother did) may read the Bible through rural glasses. That was helpful for town and country churches. Even great city churches, filled with rural refugees, got by with it, building on nostalgia. Charles L. Allen, in the center of Houston, Texas, never wearied his urban congregation and television audience with his stories of tiny country churches in rural Georgia.

The city life of the Bible can be read and proclaimed, too. After all, it was in Jerusalem that Jesus was tried and crucified amid the tugs of complex political intrigue. Our Lord was a builder. Construction images of plumb lines and squares and levels, business references to honest weights and measures, and allusions to foreign armies and political pressures saturate the scriptures—stuff of the city.

Think of Christianity's spread. When we read the New Testament through urban eyes, the book of Acts throbs with city life. Paul was converted on the way to Damascus, perhaps the oldest continually inhabited city in the world. He was baptized on one of the busiest market streets in the world, the street called "Straight." They were first called Christians in the metropolis of Antioch. Barnabas and Paul set out for Ephesus and Thessalonica. Paul preached where philosophers smoked their pipes on Mars Hill in Athens, and he witnessed from a prison cell in Rome. He wrote his letters to churches in the great cities of the Roman Empire—Corinth and Ephesus and Philippi. Images of travel, trade, mixed populations, armies, mobile populations, and racial and religious persecution spring from the biblical text.

It can very well be argued that Christianity was born in the city. The Word of God is for all people, and the saving work of Christ is aimed at the human heart, rural or urban. Even so, we can still rejoice that, as we face the urbanization of the world, we have a book filled with urban experiences.

John Wesley was a missionary evangelist out of place in rural Epworth, England. His mission targeted the displaced people of the industrial revolution. When he said, "The world is my parish," he sounded more like Billy Graham in one of his crusades than he sounded like a rector in Suffolk.

Wesley preached to the coal miners, taught industrial and shipyard workers in Bristol, gathered children in London into schools, and set up class meetings in Cardiff, Wales. The Wesleyan revival in England was a spiritual penetration of the city.

In contrast, the church in England organized a geographic "parish" system, George G. Hunter III reminds us. A vicar served the parish church and assumed responsibility for the farms within a certain radius. The parish system served medieval Britain well. Rural people were scattered fairly evenly throughout the land.

But the Industrial Revolution tore millions of people from their farms and drove them to mines and factories. The church, just like today, built a few additional churches in the cities, but never seriously and strategically deployed its ministers or its resources to deal with the massive shift to urban population centers. Many of our denominations in the United States have pursued a similar plan in the twentieth century.

A Different Way of Thinking

The funny thing about the rural mindset is that most farmers don't hold it anymore. Only town and city folks with long, selective, and somewhat romantic memories do. Farm people don't sing "over the meadow and through the woods, to Grandmother's house we go." They catch a flight to Denver to see their grandkids for the weekend, eat fast foods, and follow their favorite teams on the tube.

For the purposes of our discussion, let me compare what I choose to call a nineteenth-century set of rural values to a near twenty-first-century set of urban values. I believe that the mainline churches have never moved to town. We are living eighty years behind the times.

For better or worse, America—for that matter, the entire world—is now urban. That means a contrasting culture and an altered approach to ministry. Look at the differences.

Alike—Diverse

In the old days in a farm town in Minnesota whose population was mostly of Swedish or Norwegian descent, you would likely have attended the Lutheran church. In a German community, the population may have been part Roman Catholic, part Lutheran. Most folks in the church enjoyed a similar life-style.

But city life is diverse. I stepped on an elevator in our small city of Little Rock the other day. Four people got on with me—a banker of Japanese descent, a black attorney, and two bank directors who spoke in different regional dialects, one Midwestern and the other Southern. Normal life in the city.

How can churches minister to a melting pot of humanity? Alive churches do these things: They preach the Christ who "breaks down the wall of hostility" and they practice grace, remembering that "God is no respecter of persons." City churches demonstrate diversity.

Churches who think in modern terms establish varieties of fellowship, worship, and ministry. The chancel choir sings Mozart at 11:00 A.M., the singles ensemble sings contemporary songs at 8:30 A.M. The Korean congregation worships in the chapel at 2:00 P.M.

Diversity dictates the social scene. People work shifts at the factories, weekends and nights at the hospitals, rotation on the police force. Growing churches worship on Saturday and Wednesday nights. The Roman Catholic Church, more familiar with urban ways, led the way with Saturday night mass at 5:00 P.M. and communion each morning. In Korea, Bible study and prayer fellowships meet in office buildings, banks, schools, and factories at practically all times of the day or night.

We once designated 11:00 A.M. on Sunday for worship. That's a great time, but it's not the only time. Early Sunday morning services are immensely popular for some city folks, particularly if a full choir participates. Saint James Church in Little Rock averages sixty in worship on Saturday evenings. That's bigger than half the churches in America. They follow that with three services on Sunday morning, after an early singles' breakfast.

Diversity means a "target" ministry. Unless you want to limit Christianity to middle class families, ask yourself where are the people and where is the pain. John Wesley said, "Go to those who need you. Go first to those who need you most." Who are they? Forty to forty-five percent of the adult population is single, but that's not sharp enough. What kind of singles? Unmarried in their twenties? Hispanic? Working people? Divorced? Young parents? Widowed, in their sixties? Carry it further—can you minister to street people? The university community? Teenagers? What about the firemen and their families? Without being crass, businesses must pinpoint their marketing, striving for a niche in the market. Amid a diversity of humanity, the church has to aim specifically and carefully to meet personal needs. Jesus had a proclivity for pinpointing specific personal needs.

The miracle of the gospel is that the greater the spiritual

power, the more diverse the fellowship can be. When Peter witnessed the Holy Spirit come upon Cornelius, he was convinced that Gentiles belonged in the church. In an Alcoholics Anonymous meeting, where lives are being changed, the lawyer and the construction worker can weep and laugh together. A powerful dose of Christ's love will overcome diversity. When people are still "in the world," they are frightened, provincial, insecure, and divisive.

Congregations start new fellowships for distinct groups who need a "port of entry" and special nurture. Mothering churches start congregations with language groups, racial groups, and economically disparate groups in an effort to reach the unchurched.

Leaders of denominations devise congregations that are theologically different throughout the city. Determine your parameters—that is, how broad your theological arms care to reach—then diversify. Shape one church toward praise, healing, and warmth; another church toward social service and justice ministries; another with liturgy and quiet dignity; and another with serious Bible study and evangelical fervor. The task makes personnel placement maddening, but the city requires it. The Roman Catholic and Episcopal churches have exemplified flexibility, especially with charismatic and healing groups. A denomination must decide how far it can stretch, but diversity is essential.

So also a local church must decide how broad, how caring, and how diversified it will be. Is there room for speaking in tongues in your church, even in a prayer group? A hand raised? An amen? A teardrop on the carpet? A prayer at the communion rail? In Spanish? Is there a planned place for divorced people? For youth?

The Bible tells us that the blood of Christ breaks down barriers, for example, between Jew and Gentile, between men and women, between slave and free. I've always wanted to ask a congregation how many barriers they want God to break down. How much of the blood of Christ do they desire?

No longer can we talk to preachers about $20,000 or $30,000 churches, referring to a salary bracket, as if we had a cookie cutter operation. It takes a wedding of unique congregations and particular pastoral personalities to make a ministry work in the city.

Look at the distinctive, long-range pastoral ministry of Ed Beck in Colorado Springs. Ed says:

> Sunrise is a western life-style church. Our worship services are with dignity, but they are laid back. During prayer time personal needs are shared openly and all persons hold hands as the church prays. We state to our visitors that we hope they will not be offended as someone reaches over and holds their hand. It is a symbol of our need to be reached, too, our need to reach out and the assurance that God reaches us.
>
> We find that over one-third of our visitors come through the yellow pages. . . . All of our visitors are called by phone Sunday afternoon beginning at 1:30 P.M. They are all visited, depending on feedback of the phone conversation, within no later than forty-eight hours. Each visitor unit/family receives a small loaf of bread—we call it the symbol of the "Bread of Life."
>
> We have holistic (healing) services once a month and will soon go to once a week. The anointing of oil and praying for [wholeness] is an idea here whose time has come!
>
> We have grown a little over 200 per year for the last several years. We are now at 900 plus members. We plan to be 3,500 members within 8 to 10 years.

Small—Big

City people do not fear bigness; they revel in it. Try to get a ticket to the Boston Celtics game; eat Sunday brunch atop the World Trade Center building; ask a cabbie in Chicago or Atlanta which city has the busiest airport. Cities think big.

In religious terms, *big* is neither holy nor unholy. The same is true for *little*. Jesus fed the 5,000, and he ate the Last Supper with 12. The plumb line of God demands faithfulness, regardless of the social scene. Put a limit on ego trips, but don't put a limit on God. The fact is that most of the world's people live in cities, where big is the order of the day.

Small was normal and nice in rural nineteenth-century America. Neighbors came to church and called everybody by name. "Isn't Susie growing up to be a young lady?" "I'll bet that boy will be a big help before long." Drinking coffee at the town cafe or picking up the mail at the post office always included a visit with friends.

The city is big, thinks big, likes big. When I'm in the big city, I stare up at the skyscrapers. When I fly into New York or Atlanta at night, I think of all the people behind all the lights and wonder what is going on in their homes and apartments. Five billion people live on the planet, and the number is still growing.

Dr. Sundo Kim asked me to preach one Sunday in Kwang Lim Church in Seoul at 7:00 A.M., 9:00 A.M., 11:00 A.M. and 2:00 P.M. The sanctuary seats 4,300 people, and Sunday after Sunday it is filled to overflowing at almost every service. I felt the presence of God at Kwang Lim Church. In Seoul, ten million people live and work. Thirty years ago, 5 percent of the people were Christians; today 25 percent are Christians. The question is not: "What system do you like personally?" The question is: "How can we reach the multitudes for Christ?"

City churches think big; the city demands it. I like the words of the great Elton Trueblood: "Whatever else our Lord had in mind, it is clear that he envisioned something very big."

In the 1970s in the United States, there was a shift to an almost unapologetic boldness in the building of large churches, especially by new, independent congregations. The number of churches with 2,000 people attending each week increased from a mere dozen to more than 100 by 1984. Today, the number is closer to 200. Only a handful are mainline churches.

Large churches develop wild and wonderful styles of urban Christianity. A building cannot contain some congregations. Highland Park Baptist Church in Chattanooga, Tennessee—an independent Baptist church with 57,000 members—has approximately 60 satellite chapels. "The greatest problem in the worldwide missionary work of the church," writes John N. Vaughan in *The Larger Church*, "may well be the problem of how to provide pastoral care to millions."

The really big churches are overseas according to Vaughan. The Jotabeche Methodist Pentecostal Church in Santiago, Chile—a mother church and forty satellite groups—has more than 80,000 members. The Yoido Full Gospel Church of Seoul has nearly 500,000 members and is still growing, aided by 19,839 cell groups, 316 members of the pastoral staff, and 20,805 elders, deacons, and deaconesses. The congregation has three satellite ministries in Korea and has planted 118 churches outside Korea. "Brazil for Christ" reportedly is constructing the world's largest sanctuary, seating 25,000.

In the Soviet Union, First Baptist Church of Moscow has a combined attendance of 5,000 each Sunday. A Church of God congregation in Port-au-Prince, Haiti, averages 3,000 to 5,000 each Sunday. In Shanghai, a city of 12 million, the Protestant Mo'en Church has 6,000 in three Sunday services.

The styles of ministry vary. The Baptists emphasize the Sunday school. Brazilian and Chilean Pentecostals have home groups, giant sanctuaries, and satellite chapels. The Koreans emphasize cell groups and class meetings in the homes, daybreak prayers, and huge sanctuaries with multiple worship services.

The key seems to be large worship celebrations combined with intensive decentralization. More than half of the largest congregations in the world have a number of satellite groups. Lots of leaders are needed, right down to a class meeting of three people. Paul Cho insists that "when any church adopts this system of home cell groups, it is going to grow."

When Jesus saw the city, he wept. "If even now you knew the things that make for peace." On another occasion, "he saw a great throng, and he had compassion on them, because they were like sheep without a shepherd; and he began to teach them many things" (Mark 6:34). It's high time we "see" the cities, weep over the cities, and begin to teach them many things. We will need to think big; we will need church centers; we must penetrate apartments, trailer courts, office buildings, and houses.

In the foreseeable future, we will need church buildings. But the power of growth, I believe, will be where people eat and sleep. To reach millions of people, we have the same resource the early Christians had: the homes. I believe that if Christians would surrender their living rooms to God, we could evangelize the world.

We ought to fear unfaithfulness and pride and prostitution of the gospel—but not a preconceived notion of bigness.

Some religious groups believe that only 144,000 people will go to heaven. Apparently, they don't want to see heaven crowded. But God has managed to create billions of stars, with space enough to go between them. The planet is big enough for people to be converted and to find and serve God and one another. Heaven can handle it. Think big.

Stationary—Mobile

The rural church is tied to the land. Some folks reminisce about the "little country church where I was baptized." Some people won't join a new fellowship when they move to the city. They want to keep their roots "back home."

This attitude is understandable. The country church was a kind of fortress where people banded together to fight the elements, link arms against tragedy, and push back the angel of death. By their own sweat and tears they built churches dedicated to God in spite of drought, depression, or disease. They quarried the stone, crafted the prayer rails, and cooked the dinners. The church building symbolized their sacrifices and their spiritual roots.

But the city is on the move. Populations shift. Robert Schuller of the Crystal Cathedral says that if we were in the grocery business and our churches were stores, we would tear down 90 percent of our buildings, redesign them, and recon- struct them where the people are. We would sell a lot more groceries.

Many a church building ought to be torn down or sold, the congregation relocated, and love of the building transferred to love of the Savior. The more we care about people, the more mobile we have to become.

City people travel. Except for the very poor, they go anywhere they want to go. They drive to the football stadium, take the subway to the baseball game, and have lunch across town. They worship where their friends worship. City people don't ask how far; they ask how many minutes—or they don't ask at all. They just decide whether they want to go.

Paul Cho's church, with nearly half a million members, doesn't have any parking. But he's located at the hub of Seoul's magnificent subway. People pour in by the thousands.

Remaining stationary instead of having mobility affects the way we minister. A pastor friend is having a miserable time doing pastoral calling in the city. He jumps in his car, just the way he did in the village, and sets off to make calls. The first family is not home. He can't locate a house on a tucked away street. The apartment complex is locked. One man, just home from third shift, is sleeping and doesn't come to the door. A woman, inconvenienced by his unannounced visit, asks him to come back. He returns to the church exhausted, frustrated, and angry, thinking that people don't care about God or the church. His structure for ministry does not match the life-style of the city.

In a mobile world, people organize life differently. They make appointments. They use the telephone, the radio, and T.V. They gather at convenient places. They meet for lunch or near where they work. They go where they have mutual interests. A seven-day-a-week church can be a dynamic place to meet. One evangelistic pastor helps people prepare to join the church by scheduling appointments in his office.

Lay members at Southport United Methodist Church in Indianapolis, Indiana, spend every Sunday afternoon and Monday evening calling on worship visitors. Each week every visitor is contacted. Many of those who call speak seriously and significantly about their faith and the church. The people they visit have been surprised and pleased. Some laity and pastors achieve this goal by telephoning, with additional telephone calls being made by Sunday school teachers or choir directors.

Most city dwellers go to places they enjoy. They follow their commitments. A singles group will plan for three months to go skiing or build an orphanage in Honduras or work at the city's Thanksgiving dinner for the poor. They're mobile. The church needs to think mobile, too.

Stability—Change

Traditional rural life had a rhythm, a seasonal pattern, a daily routine. Change meant severe storms, epidemics, and economic depression. Church life provided strength with familiarity and stability. Some rural churches now have a defensive stance as they battle to stay alive. Change appears malevolent. Many young pastors hit a brick wall when they propose new ideas. Some people have a theme song: "Come well or come woe, my status is quo."

In the city, change is the accepted way of life. Stores close; new stores open. Thoroughways wipe out entire residential districts. A neighborhood changes nationalities or color or language. Factories hire thousands, then suddenly close. Continually changing strategies govern aggressive, vital church life. Women are working; they can't organize church fundraisers anymore. Who is going to raise money for missions? If they believe in the project, they'll figure out a way to finance it. Youth go to school in the morning, work at jobs in the afternoons, and study or party at night. When will they come to church? They'll come if it's meaningful. Singing or praying or sharing is refreshing and revitalizing. Weekend retreats draw youth. So can work camps in the summer. Prayer and study groups in colleges often meet in dorms or fraternity houses at 11:00 P.M.

Churches ministering to single adults vary the program. Doug Morphis, of First UMC in Wichita, has 250-300 single adults for TNT—Thursday Night Together. A plethora of classes, lasting about six weeks at a time, attract various interests. Then new classes and fresh subjects emerge, everything from "cooking for one" to a study of John's Revelation.

The population shifts suddenly, dramatically. Leaders need to be alert to new urban developments. Like a city planner, a superintendent or missionary secretary needs to study urban developments, school district proposals, new industry starts, and utility designs. City missionary groups must be thinking and planning all the time. We ought to be as aggressive as secular developers are. We especially need to target the economic underbelly, the working poor, minority groups, and the destitute.

Change for people means uprooting of spiritual moorings as well as a physical move. Loss of a job, a transfer of cities, a divorce, the death of a parent or spouse—all are opportunities to offer the grace of Christ and the fellowship of the church. In life's disjunctures, people are in need of friends and are unusually receptive to God.

In rural areas, residents are often classified in mental concrete as "churched" or "unchurched." Old-timers say, "No use calling on the Smiths. We knew his granddaddy and his daddy. They were never interested in the church." New residents may be considered "outsiders" and denied leadership roles in the congregation.

But move the family to town and attitudes change. Nobody knows. They are open to new ideas, new faces, and new friends. New congregations, new classes, new study groups are especially effective in touching relocated people. I have baptized many an adult who would never have entered the doors of the church "back home."

This "stability-change" idea relates to the tenure of pastors. In the old days, rural church life could be boring, especially if the preacher lacked imagination or education. Having a new preacher every year or two was helpful. Everything else stayed the same, so a new voice was refreshing.

But in the city, people's lives are being torn up; disruption is the order of the day; movement is constant. Pastors need to stay. One preacher said, "My congregation is moving. I might as well stay put." In an uprooted society, something needs to be grounded.

The Board of Homeland Ministries of the United Church of Christ gave special awards to two churches recently. Notice the tenure of the pastors.

Trinity UCC in Chicago is a "spirit-filled church" and "unapologetically Christian and unashamedly black." The Reverend Jeremiah A. Wright has led the congregation from 70 members in 1972 to 4,200 members now. At present, 18 members are enrolled in seminaries. Trinity will be his life's work.

Church of the Beatitudes UCC in Phoenix, a city defined by mobility, has grown 100 members a year since its founding in 1954. Reverend Culver H. Nelson has been its only pastor, building the congregation to over 3,200 members, constructing a campus for the 750 elderly on a 25-acre development.

Learning from Urban Churches

Many people in small churches are turned off by big churches. "We don't want to be like that," they say. But churches of all sizes, town and country alike, ought to pick up tips for more effective ministries. As I have urged, we're all living in an urban world now.

A church in the city must approach the task in the same way a missionary does in a foreign land. Not long ago, I was invited to "listen in" on a retreat led by Peter Druecker, the well-known management consultant. Druecker guided 20 pastors of metropolitan churches through in-depth discussions of leadership. Most of these preachers were from independent community churches involving over 2,000 people in worship. Believe me, they understand "the secular city."

I drank a cup of coffee with the Reverend Rick Warren of Saddleback Church in the Saddleback Valley, south of Los Angeles. He was dressed in designer jeans, a California sport shirt and sweater, and looked about thirty-five-years-old. He was really "California laid back."

"Tell me about your church," I said to him.

"Well, it's more of a movement than it is a church. Nine years ago I picked the Saddleback Valley to begin a new church because of the high level of education and the low level of church participation. Put a secular college education and a long distance from home roots together, add the mountains on one side and the sea on the other, and you have a world where church is not very important."

"What did you do?" I asked.

"The first thing was to go house to house asking questions of the unchurched. Who were they? What were their needs? Why did they think most people didn't go to church? What would they look for in a church? Then I began to design a strategy. We rented a school, began to send out mailings, and tried to deal with questions people were asking. With our first converts we began teaching the Scriptures in the homes. Then we would slowly ask our members to open their homes and invite and teach others. I began to train lay leadership."

I asked, "How many of those groups do you have now?"

"Oh, about 150 or so," he answered. "They are led by lay pastors."

"Lay pastors?" My surprised look made him smile.

"They're not ordained. I commission them, but. . . . " Then he became very serious. "They invite, they teach, they counsel, they break bread together. They bring converts on Sunday morning and assist me in baptizing them. They do practically everything our ordained pastors do." He turned to me and asked, "Didn't you Methodists once have class meetings?"

"Yes," I admitted, "a long time ago."

"Well, that's sort of what we're trying to do."

"Don't your groups go off in all directions?"

"No, I meet with the leaders on a regular basis. I teach them the Scriptures, we talk and pray. That weekly contact—that's very important to them. They don't miss. You see, they have responsibility for ten or twelve people. Sometime I think pastors are so afraid of wildfire that they run around stomping out every little campfire that could warm up their churches."

"Tell me about your church building," I said.

"We meet in a high school. We are talking about building some day, but we're in no hurry. One of our church's foundational principles is 'build up before building out.' Most churches build too soon and too small. Then they are stuck. We've grown from zero to 4,000 by renting thirteen different buildings over the years. We don't harp on 'money' either. That's the number one complaint on non-church people. We teach the tithe and work with whatever we receive. What we're really trying to do is to train people to live a Christian life. We use the campus and the homes as training locations to help people enter into the walk with the Lord. Then we put them in ministry to others. My goal is to turn yuppies into 'yummies' (young urban professional into young urban missionaries)."

Our informal time was almost over. I said, "You are sitting here relaxed, visiting with me. Yet, you have spiritual responsibility for over 4,000 attenders each Sunday and have begun thirteen churches in nine years. How do you do it?"

"Group life," he replied thoughtfully. "A church must grow larger and smaller at the same time. We multiply groups. Of course, I still personally minister to many places of need, but you'd be surprised how many people are sustained by their home groups, their lay pastors, their Sunday school classes, their various lay ministries. I teach and train, even in preaching. The pastor is supposed to 'build up the body,' not carry it on his or her shoulders. People who love the Lord can help each other if they're built into community."

I thought about the early Christians. They devoted themselves to the apostles' training, to the breaking of bread, to the fellowship and prayers . . . "and they distributed to them all as any had need."

Go into a Korean church and visit the "post office." That's right, most vestibules are equipped with a myriad of slots, all named. One half-inch slot per member is just big enough for the tithe booklet, the worship bulletin, and any personal notes the pastor or someone might care to write. The member takes the tithe booklet (which reminds me of a savings and loan passbook), puts the weekly tithe in it, then places the whole thing in a huge, deep offering bag.

I asked several Korean pastors how many members actually tithed. They responded about the same—70 percent or 80 percent. Some husbands who were not Christians would not let their wives tithe; some were out of work; and so on. Can you imagine how energized our churches would be with that level of giving? Jesus indicated that our enthusiasm follows our money rather than the other way around. "Where your treasure is, there will your heart be also" (Matt. 6:21). Too many American church people are like the person who, as he was immersed, held his billfold up out of the water.

Here's the point of the Korean mailboxes: Pastors, Bible Women, and lay leaders know at a glance immediately after church who was absent, and they begin their calling.

Dal Joon Won, a Korean minister and friend, says that it is not unusual for a pastor, a Sunday school teacher, a lay leader, and a class leader to call the following week to see what was wrong with the absentee. Attendance is taken for granted. Absence is cause for concern. Contact on each absentee is made immediately. How's that for accountability?

In the city, accountability is difficult. It's too easy for

someone to slip through the cracks. Our most aggressive churches wait three or four weeks before telephoning absentees. Books on reclaiming inactive members, like *Caring About Inactive Members* by Oman Stuenkel, urge that good attendance records be kept and prompt contact be made. "When someone has not communed for some time, a call is made." What a contrast to the Korean accountability. Unfortunately in some churches, pastors allow the membership to grow cold. They don't know people's addresses, and married names are not learned. Then, with an air of smugness years later, names are taken off the rolls by church action. We call them "dead," but they are alive, lost to the church by sloppy pastoral and congregational care.

The church that conquers the city will have built-in methods to express weekly concern for each member.

Here's another urban design.

Brownsville, Texas, is not a huge city. It lies on the United States side of the Rio Grande; Matamoros lies on the Mexico side. Brownsville presents a dramatic mix of Anglo and Hispanic, new money and old money, new poverty and old poverty, longtime residents and newcomers. In the winter, throw in a big batch of northern winter residents who don't speak either "Texan" or Spanish. How do you make strategies for the proclaiming of the gospel in such a diverse population mix with so many complex issues?

A few years ago, the congregation of First United Methodist Church there tackled the task, knowing only a few words of Spanish and a great compassion for people. Like the proverbial chicken and the egg, it's hard to say which came first, church growth or missional outreach. The congregation's approach to evangelism is to urge—really urge—the laypeople to invite their friends, their working associates, and their neighbors to church. At the same time, they started to work with low income Hispanics. Two young doctors, one married to a Hispanic, the other a former Peace Corps volunteer, were drawn into the fellowship. Jim Pace, former missionary to Bolivia, pitched in, adding his fluent Spanish and commitment to social justice to the team.

The church struck hard with a one-two punch. They reached out to second and third generation Hispanics who spoke

English in their homes, and genuinely opened the fellowship. The original members of the church began to realize that some of their best friends, business associates, and longtime neighbors were lapsed Hispanic Roman Catholics. Prejudices run deep, but Christ's grace penetrated the fellowship.

Equally difficult was the missional outreach to the very poor, Spanish-speaking neighbors in the colonias. Health care needs are immense in Matamoros, so the church formed two health clinic/preaching stations. Their young doctors volunteered time, and lay pastors served the preaching points. After a time, two chapel/clinics received a full-time pastoral appointment.

On the Brownsville side, in cooperation with Rio Grande Conference structures, First Church "mothered" the "Southmost Iglesia Metodista." A First Church contractor built the small building, and the church helped support the lay pastor. Now forty to fifty attend worship regularly.

Given dedicated leadership and a flexible approach, the Holy Spirit can make breakthroughs even in a location that is as diversified in language, culture, and economics as Brownsville. It shows that a local church can lead, and cooperate, with denomination structures, even across national boundaries.

Are you ready for two illustrations from dramatically different congregations in the same city? Consider Hennepin Avenue UMC and Park Avenue UMC in Minneapolis. Hennepin, with a historically articulate pulpit, stirs the mind on great issues of the day; yet, it provides a personal side to the gospel as well. Pastor David T. Scoates has brought a new dynamic program. Young singles flock to it. Care for people who have handicapping conditions means the installation of wheelchair ramps, elevators, wireless aids for the hearing impaired, and large print editions of Bibles, hymnals, even bulletins.

Outreach social service at Hennepin includes a large counseling center across the street; a retreat and conference center an hour away; a "Steeple People" store two blocks away, where one hundred volunteers sort, repair, and sell used clothing at low cost; and a "Loaves and Fishes" ecumenical ministry that provides free meals to street people. Notice the varied responses to human need, the willingness to think big, and the use of many lay volunteers. Hennepin also projects high visibility in this city of a million people with an elaborate Christmas pageant (but then not every church has a former Walt Disney executive to produce its pageants!).

Now go into the inner city on the south side of town. Park Avenue saw the inner city go from being a middle income neighborhood in the 1920s to a low income neighborhood in the 1940s. It was difficult to receive people of the new neighborhood into the ever dwindling congregation. Barriers of class and race kept them apart.

Reverend Phil Hinerman gave a quarter century to the task. He began by tearing down a house and building a parking lot. The people would not come inside. So, like Whitefield, he went outside. He used summer programs, tents, high powered celebrities, nationally known Christian musicians, and top youth evangelists to reach a thousand people a night during summer services.

They hired highly committed students from nearby Christian colleges as youth workers—fifty of them in the summer, three year round. They have developed a powerful ministry, primarily with black children of the neighborhood. Six thousand children between the ages of five and eighteen live within one mile of the church. Demographics show that 90 percent are from broken homes and that 80 percent are black.

The target area has been the youth, now over 1,300 in the summers and several hundred year round. For the ghetto, they do way out things: backpacking in the mountains, work camps, bicycle trips, strenuous hiking, sports of all kinds, even survival training.

Lo and behold, black people began to come inside. Gospel messages, prayer at the altar, strong Bible teaching, and contemporary gospel and spiritual music drew people of all walks of life. Men and women—scores of them across the years—stepped forward to enter missions, ministry, and youth work. Now over 20 percent of the worshiping congregation is black, and the love inclusiveness factor is high. The saving work of Christ is preached, experienced, and is breaking down the walls of hostility. Now Robert Stamps carries on the work as pastor.

I fear that small churches will write these illustrations off as gigantic enterprises beyond their capabilities. Don't do it. A little church in a town with a population of 800 in the Kansas wheat fields operates an "Econ Shop" just as Hennepin Avenue does. They use forty volunteers during the year and earn thousands of dollars for missions. Like Park Avenue, a half dozen little churches cooperate to hire a summer youth worker, involving forty or fifty kids in dynamite summer activities. The program includes a work camp, a spiritual retreat in the mountains, a Vacation Bible School, and a youth revival in which commitments are made and lives are changed. One small city church has a family therapist on staff one-half day a week. A little mission church in the city is the site for a "stone soup" meal every Sunday noon to serve hungry street people.

I was proud of a young pastor of several small congregations in Georgia. He caught the spirit. "I started meeting with the twelve youth on Sunday evenings, many of whom had no ties with any of the churches. One of these new youths is now in my confirmation class."

God is at work in the city, but a fast-paced, flexible, highly mobile, urban style of ministry must be operative. We can move Christian fellowship from the farm to the town if we will put our minds to it. After all, the sons and daughters and the grandsons and granddaughters of some of those farm folks are now in "Detroit City."

We are fifty years overdue in making the transition from rural thinking to city thinking. To transform our mindset to urban culture and bend our systems to reach metropolitan people will require a great obedience to the gospel. It will necessitate a wrenching of the will.

Ezekiel understood that God rode along in the chariots as they rolled from Judah to Babylon. Remember the eyes of fire in the wheels within the wheels? Well, God can also race down the freeways of Los Angeles and visit Queens in Southside Manhattan.

Just ten years ago, there were 160 cities in the world with populations over one million. By the year 2000, over 500 cities will exceed one million. When Harvey Cox wrote *The Secular City*, he made it clear that the whole world had become in the twentieth-century one immense metropolis. Any church that intends to take the gospel to the people in the future will have to tackle the city. It will need to welcome change, be mobile, think big, and accept diversity. Like Nicodemus, the historic rural churches must be born anew.

CHAPTER FOUR

Soul Hungers

What are the soul hungers of our society? Where do people bleed? How will your church touch the wounds with healing?

Basically, people are the same in all generations—deep down. The Bible reminds us that we are alienated, separated from God. The cast of characters in the Bible can walk off the pages any day and play out their lives on our city streets.

> Judas still haggles at his wares,
> Cain is forever new-created!
> Delilah, in a Paris frock,
> Goes out to tea at five o'clock;
> Salome climbs the Subway stairs,
> Potiphar takes the Elevated!
> (from "Sic Transit"
> by Sara Henderson Hay)

In the kaleidoscope of our confused self-centeredness, each turn of the wheel brings fresh patterns of pain and passion. Each era shows certain symptoms, specific soul hungers. What are ours? Like a physician, how can we say, "Thou ailest here . . . and here?"

Our Committee on Membership asked a prominent New York firm that studies cultural values and tries to look ahead a few years to help us. Companies hire these firms to describe what consumers will want five years from now—trying, I suppose, to avoid building another Edsel. Breakfast food manufacturers try to find out whether moms and dads want fiber or toys in their children's breakfast cereal.

Our committee wanted to know what Americans, particularly adults under the age of forty, were searching for in their spiritual lives. Here's what we learned: Americans are looking for three things—values, meaning, and intimacy.

Values

Americans are searching for values. Baby boomers, those people born for a decade or so after World War II, struggle to sort out what is good—good for themselves, good for their families. They want significant jobs, healthy foods, and clean air. They're shopping all the time. True, they focus on "I," but they are looking.

It isn't an easy task. Alvin Toffler, in *Future Shock*, reminds us that we make our choices in a "Baskin Robbins" world. A thousand decisions face us daily. What is good or bad is not always clear. There are too many shades of gray. How do we really know what is good for us? Who can we trust?

The task is especially difficult because values have not been taught as they were in the past. Even college graduates lack backgrounds in classic literature, philosophy, and history, which weigh the difference between good and evil. Neither do they know the Bible. Alan Bloom states in his book *The Closing of the American Mind* that students used to know something about Moses and the law and about Jesus and his preaching. "Passages from the Psalms and the Gospels echoed in children's heads," he writes. But today, he insists, Jews and Christians alike have neglected the book that tells them what is right and wrong, good and bad, and explains why they are so.

What we have is a self-oriented "me first" generation that looks rather pleadingly for whatever would be good for them. But they have little guidance.

Habits of the Heart sums it up. In our society, "the individual can only rarely and with difficulty understand himself and his activities as interrelated in morally meaningful ways with those other different Americans. Fragile communities are put together to meet utilitarian . . . needs of individuals, with only peripheral survival of older biblical and republican themes."

Tradition doesn't cut much ice either. Just because Dad was a Nazarene or Mom was a Catholic, they want to go where their needs will be met. Remember when folks were loyal to a brand? "I'm a Chrysler man"—meaning you'll only see a Dodge or Plymouth in my driveway. Or "My farm is green"—always John Deere tractors and implements in the field. Presbyterians used to be like that. Catholics, too. And Greek Orthodox. But no more. Talk about ecumenical: The Consultation on Church Union (COCU) may be dead in the water at the national level, but in Detroit or Seattle, Mennonites merge with Methodists, and Roman Catholics and Baptists convert to the Fellowship Bible Church.

Many United Methodist pastors tell me that less than half of their membership are United Methodist in background. Many members are new converts. They come from all over the world. They're exploring biblical values and are not much interested in labels.

Some new churches, like Saddleback Church in the Silicon Valley of California, play down their denominational ties until folks get settled. Completely loyal to the Southern Baptist Convention, they just don't want to scare strangers away with trademarks. Quapaw Quarter Church in Little Rock omits the denominational label on its big billboards. The United Methodist name comes later. Joe and Mary Smith are going to shop around. They'll stop in, look it over, feel it out.

That's why I'm enthusiastic about invitational evangelism. Invite people to participate in your fellowship before being concerned about their membership. Whether you call it "relational evangelism" or "hospitality evangelism" or "centripedal ministries," the object is to help people experience the fellowship and interest with the quality of life. Debbi Fields, founder and president of Mrs. Fields Cookies, Inc., didn't sell a single cookie the first morning she was in business. Then she gave out free samples, and her multimillion dollar cookie business took off. If we have something good in the church, let people taste it. "Come and see," invited Jesus.

I was pleased to receive this letter from Reverend Royal Speidel, one of the pastors of the Chicago Temple:

> I found your candor refreshing.
>
> I appreciated particularly your reversing our common approach to evangelism. At the Chicago Temple I have trained and brought in over 1,000 new members over the last 12 years, but many of them have disappeared in a short time. Your book has confirmed the need to get people involved first, and then to bring them into membership.

Reverend Mike Slaughter, pastor of the fast growing Ginghamsburg UMC in Tipp City, Ohio, takes the whole matter even further. Some 700 people worship there each week, but the membership is only 400. Twenty first-time families attend each Sunday, but it is hard for them to become members. The pastor invites people into his home on Wednesday night to study the Bible and learn about church membership, with the classes lasting sixteen weeks. Class members are asked to make a personal decision for Christ midway in the course after the groundwork has been laid. A few people drop out, but that doesn't bother Reverend Slaughter. "Membership is not the goal; discipleship is. We care more about them than names on a roster. . . . I don't want this to be a 'successful' church, but to be the body of Christ, a place where lives are radically changed through Christ, and people are sent out to win others." I'm not surprised that they support four missionaries in foreign lands, a prison ministry, a clothing resale shop, and send their youth on work projects all over the United States.

Vital churches invite the unchurched to eat in their homes and churches, to pray with them, to study with them, to live and bleed and die with them. People come down out of the choir loft and ask to be baptized. They sidle over to the pastor at a Sunday school party and ask about discipleship training and full membership in the church.

Good, Says Who?

What do these computer savvy seekers use for standards? What influences their decisions? To what authority do they defer?

Put these questions in perspective. In the 1940s and 1950s, if a doctor said, "We have to take your tonsils out," we had them taken out. In the university, a professor, as the term began, would ask for a research paper due in December. Students would ask questions like "How many pages do you want?" and "What happens if it is late?"

The military needed soldiers for the Korean War. They were drafted, and they fought. In the church, people assumed that the preacher knew more about the Bible than they did. Baptism and Holy Communion were familiar rituals. The pastor and the priest spoke with authority.

But in the late 1960s and early 1970s, the pendulum swung. Doctors were trying to poison people with pills, people thought, so they flocked to health food stores. Universities instructed students not to "fold, bend, or staple your computer cards." The students tore them up in little pieces and scattered them all over the deans' offices. The military said that the Vietnam war was good; some men burned their draft cards, enrolled in graduate school, or ran to Canada.

The church? In Salina, Kansas, where I was pastor, the college kids baptized one another in the fountain at the city park at midnight. They didn't ask my opinion or my help.

But today, and in the foreseeable future, America pulsates with a new beat. The pendulum has swung back—halfway. Now baby boomers feel their way through a maze of offerings, listening to the voices bombarding them from all sides and scrutinizing the options. They make choices.

People today want to be shown. They bite the nickel to see if it's real. Then they accept it or reject it. Patients consult their doctors and get a second opinion before they go under the knife. University students choose their courses, change their majors, and maybe drop out to work for a while, feeling their intellectual pulse to see if they're learning anything. Some men and women become soldiers; some don't. Churchgoers are visiting around to see if they can find a good way to live.

They know some values they want. They seek a healthy marriage, even if they've destroyed one already. They adore their children, even though they give them little time or instruction. They want healthy bodies, even if they eat or drink too much. In short, they search for the Christ who said "I came that [you] might have life, and have it abundantly" (John 10:10). But they want to know where they can find it and how much it will cost.

Will They Buy In?

People will commit to values that make sense.

Yes, people have become cynical, skeptical, suspicious. Burned by billboards, conned by a covey of TV evangelists, and blurred by the blinking lights from a thousand neon signs, they still seek values that ring true. If they find them, they are willing to lock in. Most "under forties" are not so immune to the gospel as we thought—or else they are hurting so badly for meaning and relationships that they give the church another try. Their heads are not nodding up and down affirmatively like they were in the 1950s or sideways as in the 1970s. They look you in the eye and listen, hoping for something good enough to buy into.

Even secular leaders know that people will commit to great causes today. After studying the business world, Naisbitt and Aburdeene, in *Re-Inventing the Corporation,* write: "People want to make a commitment to a purpose, a goal, a vision that is bigger than themselves." If business can cause people to commit to a better washing machine or a safer car, how much more zealously can the church ask people to give their lives to the One who is the way, the truth, and the life?

Boy, we'd better be authentic to what we believe!

What an opportunity we have for an inviting fellowship! What a moment in history for a warm, loving dialogical fellowship. What a time for a teaching church that allows discussion, questioning, and thoughtful appraisal.

What a period in history for a church to lift up the claims of Jesus Christ and ask people to lay their lives on the line for him. What a moment to offer the authority of intelligently interpreted Scripture. What a moment to offer the authority of Scripture that leads to the inner assurance of God's grace. What a moment to offer the authority of Scripture as it stands in the center of twenty centuries of Christian tradition.

Who's reaching young adults today? Churches that demand high levels of commitment—the Mormons, the Assemblies of God, and independent churches. Years ago, Dean M. Kelley in *Why Conservative Churches Are Growing* stated that he noticed that ten of the largest Christian denominations, after uninterrupted growth since colonial times, were beginning to fade. In the mid 1960s, those denominations began to lose members, not because of heavy requirements, but because the requirements were too light. "The churches are dying today not because they are merely religious, but because they are not very religious at all." He recalls our beginnings. The Wesleyans and Anabaptists, he states, were in no haste to take someone into membership. They had tests of membership that were attitudinal and behavioral rather than solely doctrinal. They had to "know the music as well as the words." They made membership conditional on continuing faithfulness; insisted that members make their life pilgrimage together in small groups, aiding and encouraging one another; and demanded that members take rigorous training and accept the discipline of the group before they had any voice in making decisions of the group.

If I were starting a new congregation in urban secular America today, I would invite people, but I would interpret what it means to say yes to Jesus. I would lift up expectations like this: To become a Christian is to become a disciple, a learner, and a member of the fellowship of Jesus Christ. The covenant community has signs and symbols. Tithers belong to the covenant community. It's as old as Abraham.

Christians need to share in a regular weekly group meeting to study God's Word. They have to help look after one another in regular gatherings of prayer.

Within that community of faith, they would search out values. What does it mean to let your yes be yes and your no be no? Can a Christian single be sexually pure? What does it mean to pray without ceasing? Is my body a temple of the Holy Spirit? Can my marriage avoid being adulterated by others? Will stripping down possessions into a simple life-style put me in ministry to the poor? Does fasting mean turning off the TV or radio? How far will I go to sustain the fellowship? Values can be captured by Christians who probe and pray together.

Meaning

Americans are starving for meaning. They don't find it in their work or in their play.

Some readers will not comprehend this striving for meaning. Artists who thrill when beauty springs from brush or pen will not. Artisans who work long after supper sanding or fine tuning will not. Parents who revel in their children's development will not. Pastors who love their work more than food will not.

But work in a department store for a few months. Type in a room packed with typists. Make airplanes; sell cars; pick up garbage; cut meat. Start watching the clock.

Sam is a mechanical engineer at the aircraft company. He feels like a small cog on a very big wheel. Jane sits at a computer terminal alongside twenty other operators. Peter works on the assembly line. When the bell rings each afternoon, they are history!

Professional people request early retirement. I am amazed by how many doctors, dentists, lawyers, and business leaders fantasize in their fifties about early retirement. Young men and women search for years, looking for a "meaningful" job.

In America today, more people are working than ever before, but the jobs do not carry for them the freight of fulfillment.

Meaning is a human necessity. We're not talking about an option, like frosting on a cookie. Meaning is bedrock to the joy of human existence.

Psychiatrist Victor Frankl learned that meaning is essential to survival. In his famous *Man's Search for Meaning*, with the sights and sounds of holocaust in the background, he wrote: "We who lived in concentration camps can remember the men who walked through the huts comforting others, giving away their last piece of bread. It is this spiritual freedom—which cannot be taken away—that makes life meaningful and purposeful." Frankl speaks of the value of creative work, the fulfillment in experiencing beauty, even the meaning that can be found in suffering. He quotes Nietzsche's words, "He who has a 'why' to live for can bear with almost any 'how.' "

Where can meaning be found? If beauty is blocked out by the brick walls of the ghetto or by the stupid sitcoms on the TV; if creative work is stifled by the monotony of the factory or the office or the home; if suffering seems senseless and without point, what is the contemporary adult to do?

Deep down, people want to make a contribution, to do something worthwhile.

Sorry about this beer illustration, but Michelob beer has spent millions of dollars addressing this problem. Do you remember their first ads from ten or fifteen years ago? Men and women were dropping in on friends on Friday night, with lights dancing in their eyes—friendship, laughter, meaning. The ads claimed: "Weekends were made for Michelob." Then, wanting to sell more beer, men and women at the end of the day doffed their hard hats, laid down the pneumatic drills, and ran from their computers: "Evenings were made for Michelob." After hours, meaning is found in Michelob.

The unmistakable point of these ads is that meaningful life begins when the bell rings, when the whistle blows, when the work day is over.

The question for the church is: Do we have an offer better than beer, better than recreation, better than drugs, better than slow suicide by TV? Do we have anything for Christians to do? Do we have work that harbors meaning? Frankly, in many church fellowships, the answer is no.

Laity and clergy play a little game. The spiritual ministries? "That's the preacher's job," say the laypeople. "Poor me, no one will help me, I'll have to do it myself," says the martyr pastor. The end result is clericalism, as stultifying in modern Protestantism as it was in medieval Roman Catholicism.

In the fourteenth century, only the priest could read the Latin Bible; only the priest could offer the sacraments; only the priest could look after the cathedral. The laity? Pray, pay, and obey. Today only the pastor can call on the sick; only the pastor can give spiritual counseling; only the pastor can do evangelism and prepare people for baptism; only the pastor can witness to the faith.

Churches that ask laity merely to "help the pastor" will not attract happy workers. But churches that give each member a chance to perform meaningful ministries will thrive. Even people in the marketplace will volunteer, if the task makes sense to them. They will put their hands to the plow.

Mouzon Biggs, pastor of the Boston Avenue United Methodist Church in Tulsa, Oklahoma, has candlelight services every Christmas Eve. This service has been broadcast on national television. They have services at 4:00 P.M., 6:00 P.M., and 11:00 P.M. The church is always packed. Dr. Biggs says that he receives lots of telephone calls before Christmas. "Do we get to light a candle?" is the most common question his church receives. "I'm looking for a service where you get to light a candle." He says that you can structure the service in many ways, but as long as you let people light a candle, you can fill the house. That's what I'm trying to say—people want a part of the action. Everybody wants to light a little candle in the darkness.

One of the saddest letters I received was from a woman named Darlene. She said she had grown up in a Methodist parsonage. "I've stayed in The [United] Methodist Church because I believe in its basic doctrine and values. When I joined the church I now belong to, I signed a card that asked what I would like to volunteer for. I eagerly checked off greeter, usher, reader, caller on the sick and the elderly. I heard not one word from any of the committees or individuals that were in charge of organizing these volunteers. It's as if they wanted names but not people."

I want to show you some churches that understand the modern need for meaning. Several of them are fast growing churches, but that can happen if you know how to let the people perform ministry. Let's go to Oklahoma.

I remember when I raised my eyebrows at a young preacher who was starting a new church in Oklahoma City. He used fresh language, called his new work "Church of the Servant," and convinced the bishop into leaving him there for over a quarter of a century. Worst of all, he said from the beginning that the preacher's job is to train the laity for their ministry. When some people were critical of his unwillingness to call on newcomers, visit shut-ins, teach the children, and attend missional task force meetings, he knew there were many traditional churches they could attend. He worked, but differently. He worked fourteen hours a day, teaching teachers, training leaders, and guiding volunteers.

As the church grew, staff were hired, always with the admonition, "You are to do nothing but train laity for their ministry."

In their new five year plan, over ninety major missional objectives were listed. Members were especially concerned that the plan represent "the unique mission that we have been given to fulfill." Call on shut-ins. Call in hospitals. Call on newcomers and visitors. Teach children. Teach youth. Teach confirmation classes. Teach adults. Teach Bible study groups. They were working Christians—laity all.

Looking at the week's calendar boggles the mind. They hold three worship services, televised at 11:00 A.M.; Overeaters Anonymous; an aerobics class; Disciple Bible study; Alcoholics Anonymous; Alateen; Arts Academy; Children's Day Out; orchestra; singles groups; all kinds of church school classes; countless task forces and training meetings—the laity are hard at it.

But watch out. If you go to Church of the Servant—you may get hooked on a missional task that you fall in love with, one that will give meaning to your life.

Move on to Arkansas.

One day in the worship service at First United Methodist Church in Little Rock the LIFT (Lay Involvement for Free Transportation) workers—over a hundred who drive the van or assist in transporting crippled or elderly people—were recognized. They carry some people to have kidney dialysis, some to doctors or clinics. Even the pastor volunteers and claims that it's fun. Here is the testimony of one seventy-five-year-old LIFT volunteer: "I can hardly wait for my day to come around. It's the most important thing I do." How's that for meaning?

In Korea, professional people give aid and advice at Kwang Lim Church on Sundays. A counseling room is set aside for doctors, another for lawyers, another for family counselors,

another for business leaders. From about 10:00 A.M. on for the
next few hours anyone, member or not, can consult privately
with a top professional layperson. Imagine a penniless woman
getting legal counsel, or a confused man receiving business
advice on Sunday from a Christian professional. Pastor Sundo
Kim says, "People can talk informally to judges or medical
professionals it would take months to see in their offices."

Stephen Ministries

Are you familiar with Stephen Ministries? It is named for
Stephen, the first Christian martyr (Acts 6), who was asked to
distribute food to the widows.

Reverend Kenneth C. Haugk, a Lutheran pastor, determined that the Christian labor force was poorly employed. He
stepped out of the pastorate and developed "Stephen Ministries," a plan for training lay Christians for compassionate
caring. The tasks may vary, depending on the gifts and graces of
the individual. Normally, ministries provide concern for the
elderly; care for the sick, particularly the hospitalized; and
friendship with grieving people following death or divorce.
Some Stephen workers become adept at hospice care.

When I was a pastor, one of my members, a nurse and a
Stephen minister, took one terminal cancer patient at a time
and gave love, prayer, and friendship right to the end. Then she
would adopt another cancer patient as her friend. A few people,
usually professionals, offer divorce therapy groups, substance
abuse counseling, or individual counseling. Since 1978, Stephen Ministries have trained over 2,000 congregations in 53
denominations. Training requires a couple of weeks for key
leaders and a year of weekly training in the local congregation. I
don't know of a church using Stephen Ministries that is not alive
with lay ministers and fresh vitality.

Glenkirk Presbyterian in Glendora, California, gives powerful testimony:

> Seven years ago while searching for a better way to stay in touch
> with the members of our growing church, we discovered the
> Stephen Series, a system of training for lay caring ministry. We

chose to use this wonderful program to enable us to provide
ongoing, one-on-one support for those in our congregation en-
during a crisis or severe difficulty in almost any area of their lives.
Since then we have trained 150 Stephen ministers. Through this
ministry our church has a practical, supportive way of helping
Christians discover and use their gifts. Our members experience
significant personal growth as they come into a deeper understanding of their Lord and the way He comforts us with His mercy
so that we can comfort others, as Paul says in Second Corinthians.

Pray for Your Mission

Now stay with me for a deeper insight. For years I walked
down the "assimilation" trail. I read books that said "Give
everyone a job," so I put new members on this commission and
that committee. They came one time. I thought church work
was the way to get people involved—but did I ever miss the
boat! Some churches have learned to put the shoe on the other
foot. Instead of asking people to serve as needs arise and instead
of focusing on housekeeping chores, they ask each new member to pray. That's it. To kneel down and ask the Lord to help
them ascertain their personal gifts and graces. They pray that
God will help them identify their personal ministry in and
through the church. Then members lay that offering on the
altar.

Here's the way it works. I arrived at Windsor Village UMC in
Houston, Texas, at 7:45 A.M. to be sure to get a seat at the 8:00
A.M. worship service. Eight years ago, the church had 25
members, but today, about 2,000 persons attend. I stayed all
day, visiting with members to hear their story.

Thirty-seven people joined the church that morning at the
11:00 A.M. service. They had been given careful training and
preparation. They were received as full members in the middle
of the service. Invitations for commitment are given at the
close. In this predominantly black church, Kirbyjon Caldwell
asks each new member to tell the congregation what his or her
ministry is going to be. It's powerful and thought provoking and
strengthens their commitment so that members become
bonded to their church. It inspires visitors and members alike.

A middle-aged man said: "I am not able to work right now, so I'm helping with our 'homeless' program, helping stock the food pantry and the clothing supply for Houston's homeless."

An elderly woman said, "My ministry is to help in the nursery. I love to care for your babies. I've had five of my own and eight grandchildren. I guess the Lord can use me in taking care of little ones."

A thirteen-year-old boy, recently baptized, bashfully said that he sings in the young people's gospel choir and is in Sunday school. Then added, "I hope to help the ushers when I can." (Young people actually do serve as helping ushers.)

A young single woman stated: "I'm an attorney. I'm active in our singles ministry, but I also want to help with our church's legal aid work on Thursday nights. That's what attracted me to Windsor Village."

It took a while—ten or fifteen minutes—to hear from each one—but what a testimony, what a moment of victory! Kirbyjon called out, and the people responded. "Much prayer—much power! Little prayer—little power! No prayer—no power!"

My heart was beating faster. Every member and visitor in that congregation knew that to belong to Windsor Village, among other things, meant to be in ministry for the Lord.

I could belong to a church like that.

Travel now to Montgomery, Alabama's Frazer Memorial. Few people understand the modern mood and the need for meaning in ministry better than senior pastor John Ed Mathison and his key associate Reverend Jack Thompson. When our son, Paul, was ready to finish seminary, I sent him to Montgomery just to see how the system works. It's upside down, compared to most churches.

"The secret of the growth of the church is the involvement of the laity in meaningful ministry," writes Dr. Mathison.

He admits that secular Americans, "me first" types, start by asking "What does this church have to offer me?" But joy comes in the transformation, causing them to ask "What can I offer in service through the church?"

Some key ideas that John Ed Mathison keeps reiterating are:

* The needs of the community are so great, the needs of the world so overwhelming, that pastors could not possibly do it all.

* We have a very small staff in this church, so we need everyone's help.

* The biblical mandate is for every Christian to be in ministry.

* You begin immediately when you enter this fellowship, not when you become a veteran.

* Who knows better than you what your gifts and graces are? You know yourself better than we do.

* God has a unique plan for your life and, therefore, a unique ministry for you to perform.

* If God doesn't inspire people to volunteer for a project or task, then we won't do it.

Before a person joins the Frazer Church, the opportunities for ministry are explained and opportunity is given to create new ministries—wherever the Lord calls that member to serve.

The pledge card represents commitment. Special commitment folders are given to youth and children, too. On the card is a place for a tithe commitment and for a financial giving program. But most of the card deals with places of ministry— over 150 now, with blanks for new ideas. It began much smaller. The new Christian or new prospective member goes home to pray. Did not our Lord say, "The fields are already white for harvest . . . *pray* therefore the Lord of the harvest to send out laborers" (John 4:35; Matt. 9:38, italics added).

When people join the church, they are immediately placed in a new member orientation group, where they are given a card on which they may indicate a commitment in the areas of worship attendance, prayer, financial giving, and volunteer ministry. I studied the card for a long time. Something was different about it. I compared it to some others from different churches. Finally it dawned on me. There were no trustees, no finance committee, no administrative board. Running the church was a different task. Saving the world was the first responsibility. All of the categories are service ministries, not offices of the congregation.

Suddenly I realized that my own conferences are sponsoring "my job" workshops—training for the laity. I looked at the list of workshops. They are all committee work. I am helping to sponsor a major training event to help laypeople learn how to keep house!

The commitment snowballs. A woman checked that she will hold babies during worship. First thing she knows, she's part of a group, praying for families by name who have small children. Next thing she knows, she's volunteering to visit the hospital to call on new babies and taking a rose to their mothers, to enroll the baby in the nursery and ask about baptism. Some of it was her idea. She's caught up in a meaningful ministry. She's been transformed from a nursery helper to a Christian woman in ministry with families of small children.

The power, says Mathison, comes when laity start dreaming the dream, enlarging their program, and imagining innovative ways of working. They press on because they own it, because God is driving them, because they do not want it to fail. But who in the world could administer a program like that? Easy answer: Laypersons who have the gift of administration. In large churches, the staff can coordinate. I believe this concept is biblically based and will work in the tiniest churches.

You'll have to read about the new member training program, the careful supervision for each task, the renewal of missional service each year, the delay of officers until February so January training can take place. But I hope you've gotten the point of each Christian's asking for God's guidance, then offering himself or herself, as did Barnabas.

Intimacy

Americans are searching for authentic friends. They are hungry for relationships that are real and want intimacy that's honest.

Earlier we discussed rural society, that wonderful social fabric where neighbors care. If your barn burns down, neighbors show up to help rebuild it. If you're sick, the lady across the road brings homemade soup. That's the country. The city can be lonely. Mobility means moving, often to a seemingly impersonal metropolitan area.

Cities—in the old days, at least—had families, clustered in neighborhoods where people often knew one another, even in New York or Chicago. But now if you're a young mother with a baby in Seattle with your closest relative in Denver, your husband on the road all week, and your next door neighbor not caring whether you live or die, you are starved for a friend.

Add to our American rootlessness the collapse of the family, and you have social chaos. For a while we bemoaned the loss of the extended family—people like aunts, uncles, grandmas, and cousins. But now the nuclear family is shot. In the 1950s we defined a family as mom and dad, two kids, a station wagon, a dog, a well manicured lawn with a barbecue grill, and a six-pack of Pepsi Cola. Now, according to census reports, there are various configurations of what a "family" is. Consider singles, single parents, second marriages, blended families, couples living together—the list goes on. The "traditional" family with its support structure is hard to find.

This truth is supported in all quarters. Alvin Toffler argues in *The Third Wave* that the breakdown of social structures causes traumatic personal loneliness. He pleads for institutions to help us build new supportive structures.

Psychiatrist M. Scott Peck comes at it differently, but just as strongly, in *The Different Drum: Community Making and Peace*. Peck calls for a priority on "community building." He believes this is our only hope for a world bent on destroying itself. Rugged individualism has a positive side—individuation, wholeness, and self-sufficiency. But it has a negative side as well—inadequacy, brokenness, and interdependency. We cannot live without community.

Those of us who grew up on a personalistic gospel—"just Jesus and me"—know how damaging and how unbiblical that idea is. John Wesley nailed it down: "There is no such thing as solitary religion."

Loneliness is like a black hole in outer space, a form of frozen silence. Loneliness sleeps on the sidewalk with the city's homeless. Loneliness blinks tears away in the bedrooms of the suburbs.

I don't know exactly how a plant feels when it is pulled up by the roots, then stuck down in the dirt somewhere. But lots of people in our mobile society have been uprooted from rural communities and transplanted to large cities. They feel frightened, friendless—like strangers in a foreign land.

Americans are not happy about their alienation, their spaced out separation. They don't know the solution, but they know the problem. From country music to pop to hard rock, they sing about the pain. What is one of our most watched sitcoms? Why, it's "Cheers." And what is the theme song? "I Want to Go Where Somebody Knows My Name."

"Cheers" is a bar. The acceptance the characters experience at the bar seems to hold a strange assortment of people together. The church offers an acceptance that holds people together with a lot more meaning than a bar. We call it *Koinonia*.

Christian Koinonia

Christians are supposed to be good at caring. Koinonia—that sharedness of life in which we belong to one another—is supposed to be our thing. It's really God's thing, bringing people who were "afar off" together in Christ.

Musical instruments in tune to the same instrument are in tune with each other. The early Christians found that the sacrificial love of Christ broke down the lonely walls of estrangement. "Now in Christ Jesus you who once were far off have been brought near in the blood of Christ. For he is our peace, who has made us both one, and has broken down the dividing wall of hostility" (Eph. 2:13-15).

Whenever the Holy Spirit crashes in on new converts, they get together. According to opinion polls, however, most Americans believe that they can be good Christians or good Jews without belonging to a church or a synagogue. That's not what the Bible declares, and it's contrary to religious experi-

ence. The early Christians were admonished to "stir up one
another to love and good works, not neglecting to meet
together, as is the habit of some, but encouraging one another"
(Heb. 10:24-25).

The ancient teacher in Ecclesiastes knew from experience
that "two are better than one. . . . For if they fall, one will lift
up his fellow; but woe to him who is alone when he falls and has
not another to lift him up. Again, if two lie together, they are
warm; but how can one be warm alone? And though a man
might prevail against one who is alone, two will withstand him.
A threefold cord is not quickly broken" (Eccles. 4:9-12).

Early Christians, alive with the Holy Spirit, shared life with
one another:

> All who believed were together and had all things in common; and
> they sold their possessions and goods and distributed them to all,
> as any had need. And day by day, attending the temple together
> and breaking bread in their homes, they partook of food with glad
> and generous hearts, praising God and having favor with all the
> people. (Acts 2:44-47)

We ought not to be surprised that "many wonders and signs
were done" in that unity. Lonely people would be drawn to that
kind of communal joy and sharing like kids to a carnival. It is
logical that "the Lord added to their number day by day those
who were being saved" (Acts 2:47).

I asked Bishop Joao Somane Machado of Mozambique how
the church deals with loneliness in his country. After all, their
social fabric is being torn asunder by revolution, refugees, and
rural immigration. People flock to cities like Maputo by
hundreds each week.

"You must understand," he responded, "the African thinks
'community.' The African never thinks 'individual'—always
communal. On Sunday, churches will be crowded, people
looking in the windows, standing in the doorways. The preacher will announce that certain people are sick, and everyone will
pray. On Tuesday, after work, the women will go to those
homes where there are sick people, and take food, eat supper,
pray, and study and sing. On Wednesday night, after supper,

the men will do the same thing. Many healings take place, and there is much joy."

I pressed him, "That might work in the village, but how can it work in the city?"

He smiled and told me of Chamanculo Church in Maputo, over 2,000 members. The name of the church means "big fire, big flame."

"The city is divided into blocks or sectors," he said. "The people in each sector go to a different home each week, preferring to go where they can pray for the sick. They also share faith and witness with neighbors, relatives, and friends whom they invite. Remember, when you lead Africans to Christ, they are so excited and so joyous, they will bring ten or twenty relatives or friends with them to the fellowship."

I was eager to see how the fast growing Methodist, Presbyterian, and Holiness churches did it in Korea, particularly in Seoul. People pour into the capital from villages and farms. Seoul now numbers ten million people. Industrialization has broken down old societal structures and has put a strain on traditional family ties. How do they find new intimacy?

Their answer: the Wesleyan class meeting. Oh, they would not let us forget morning prayers each day at 5:00 A.M. at the church or Friday night prayer meeting or Sunday worship, or men's and women's missionary fellowships, but they would stress the class meeting or the cell group. Let me tell you about Kwang Lim Church, the largest Methodist church in Korea. Class meetings ought to be the most difficult in a huge metropolitan setting.

One sector of the city is assigned to each of the ten associate pastors. Four full-time "Bible Women" assist each of these pastors. Volunteer lay leaders help. Class meetings are organized in homes throughout the city. Usually three to seven people make up a class.

Dr. Sundo Kim expects all class leaders to come to the church on Tuesday morning from 11:00 to 12:30 or Tuesday night from 8:00 to 9:30. He teaches in both times identical sessions, using the Trinity Bible study as a resource. Then the class leader is prepared for his or her group that meets in the home. Bible Women, pastors, lay elders, and lay deacons are calling constantly to see how everything is going.

Each Sunday, a report on each of the 1,700 different class meetings is printed for the congregation. Place of meeting, leader, attendance, missionary offering—all are on the computer and are reported to the congregation every week. It is a terrible thing to lose track of souls. Loneliness is a spiritual enemy. The church must attack it as if it were a disease, a mortal enemy of humankind. Group life must become normative again for all Christians, or people will continue to fall through the cracks. Class meetings were made mandatory for Korean Methodists just as they were for early British and American Methodists. John Wesley said that it was murder to allow a new convert, a babe in Christ, to die aborning without group care and instruction. Fellowship Bible churches are springing up all around us, using our own historic devices. The church of tomorrow will have standard, even obligatory, group life as its primary method for care of souls.

In the United States, we've tried to do pastoral care on a pastor-church member basis. But pastors can't run that fast. Dr. William J. Abraham, professor of evangelism at Perkins School of Theology, puts it in historical perspective in *The Coming Great Revival:* "The single greatest loss over the years within Wesleyan circles has been the abandonment of the pattern of pastoral care established in the class meetings. Unless this or a modern equivalent is restored within Wesleyan circles, renewal will be mostly cerebral and cosmetic. Without this, young converts will not develop the spiritual stamina needed to survive in the modern world."

Some growing churches stress home Bible study groups much like Wesleyan class meetings. The Baptists form Sunday school classes. Every member is expected to be in a class. There are over 200 Southern Baptist churches with 1,000 or more in Sunday school classes.

Big churches need not lose intimacy if each member is in a regular weekly fellowship gathering. It's time for pastors to make small group life an expected, normative part of church life. Say to new members, "You won't be a happy, productive

Christian in the life of this congregation unless you are an active part of one of our groups."

One student of growing churches, John N. Vaughan, suggests that each church should have three kinds of fellowship. First the larger, celebrative congregation. Second, the mid-size Sunday school or fellowship group, where "somebody knows my name." Third, a cell, a tiny hotbed of shared faith, study, and prayer, where koinonia is thicker than blood, where no pain is too great, no tear is too salty, no joy is too inexpressible not to be shared with the others.

Churches built like that have physical and emotional healings. Lives are changed; marriages are restored; and hopes are resurrected. Those churches experience signs and wonders of the New Testament variety. Lonely people have a home.

Our son Paul teaches a *Disciple* class, composed of couples. Six couples from various professions, a wide age range, and racially inclusive share the experience. After Paul's ordination, and after the reception, we went to the parsonage. At 11:30 P.M. a knock came on the door. Here was the *Disciple* Bible study class—these six couples, all of them had to go to work the next morning—all had worked that day—they had to drive across Houston, Texas, to get to his house—and here they came. They brought cake and laughter—a party ready to begin. I sat down and listened. They began to talk about an experience they had had. One of them turned to me and said, "You just can't imagine what *Disciple* Bible study has meant to us, what getting together every week means." One of them said, "I had to take tests to pass my law exam." Another one said, "My wife was sick. This group has prayed for me every day this year."

You think Americans are not hungry for that!

The church in the 1990s will be a place where people can explore what is good. If they find it, they can commit their lives to it. It will be the church where people can roll up their sleeves. In the church and in the community in the name of Christ they can find meaning for their lives as they witness, work, and serve. It will be the place where in the brokenness of the bread and in the prayers around the circle, everybody knows their names.

CHAPTER FIVE

Square One for Beginners

Square One

I'm tempted to plead for a "back to basics" movement. The phrase has a nice ring to it. It even holds a glimmer of truth. But too many mossbacks want to go backward, when God is pulling us forward. Some churches will be dragged, kicking and screaming, into the twenty-first century.

"Back to basics" calls to mind nostalgic images of the "little brown church in the vale." People sit around the piano, singing "gimme that old time religion." Try that on an eleven-year-old kid sniffing paint thinner.

Still, we do not leap forward out of a vacuum. Every revolution remembers something; every upheaval of spiritual renewal draws heavily upon the past. Every effort we make to reinvent the church will be fortified by biblical and historical rootage.

When our Lord set out to revolutionize spiritual behavior, he reached back into earlier tradition. "What is written in the law?" Jesus asked the Pharisees. Again, he insisted, "I came not to destroy the law but to fulfill it."

Any prophet today who blows a trumpet for renewal of the church first has to take a deep breath of biblical truth and historical tradition. "Leaders must understand the interweav-

ing of continuity and change" writes John W. Gardner. Re-
birthing requires remembering our roots. The basics are what
we have lost. The simple is what we must relearn. Once we
knew it, Wesleyans and Calvinists and Anabaptists and free
churches. Now we have forgotten. When John Wesley said,
"We have nothing to do but save souls" he was nailing basics to
the wall.

My engineer roommate in college, when life or studies got
screwed up, provided a sometimes helpful comment: "It's back
to square one." Images of "Monopoly" and "Sorry" and other
table games popped to mind. Return to start, back to square
one. Begin at the beginning.

Conversion

Do you remember when you found the Lord, learning only
later that the Lord had in fact found you? When was it? Where
was it? Who helped you? Were you, like C. S. Lewis, "surprised by joy"? When did you first sing with conviction "I have
decided to follow Jesus, no turning back, no turning back"?
Makes you think of Jesus calling Levi the tax collector into
discipleship, doesn't it?

One bishop recalls that when he was thirteen, he got down
on his knees on a rolled up blanket beside a fire at church camp,
and "gave his heart to Jesus." A sophisticated preacher,
teacher, and former associate of mine, growing up in a non-
churchgoing family, put his hand on the television, as the
evangelist suggested, and asked to become a Christian. He's a
little embarrassed to talk about it now, like some kid who grew
up on the wrong side of the tracks. But he's grateful for that
moment of metamorphosis. From that time on, he walked a
different path.

Bishop Quayle, flamboyant preacher and president of a
college in the prairie states, as a twelve-year-old knelt one
stormy night on an old dictionary in a weather beaten frame
school house in eastern Colorado and said yes to God. If a
journey of a thousand miles begins with a single step, when did
you take the step to start the walk with Christ and his people?

I was baptized as an infant and raised alongside my mother's
prayers and Dad's tithe in a faithful lay home. I went to church

like I attended school or came to supper; it was standard operating procedure. When I was fifteen, a young prospective preacher from a nearby college spoke to our little youth group. He said that Jesus was like the North Star: If we set the course of our lives like a ship on the seas, navigating our lives by that star, Jesus will never lead us astray. I knelt at the prayer rail and decided "Jesus, I want you to set the course of my life." It was my link to Peter and Andrew and to the simple call of Jesus to "follow thou me."

I know there is more to theology than that. Later I read Augustine, Luther, Barth, and Moltmann. But I'll always be grateful to a college student who offered me a way to begin.

Karl Barth is supposed to have said that if he had to put his theology in one sentence it would be "Jesus loves me, this I know, for the Bible tells me so." Paul Holmer, the brilliant theologian, now retired from Yale Divinity School, was once asked by a presumptuous graduate student why he believed in God. He replied profoundly, "Because my mother told me." There has to be a simple way to start.

Signs and wonders pop up continually in congregations where people have a chance to say yes to God. A faithful woman wrote, asking me what she could do. She said, "It's been so long since we've had a pastor who asked if anyone would like to unite with the church or if anyone would like to come to the altar. Couldn't we open the doors of the church every Sunday?"

I am not bragging about churches where you get "saved every Sunday." Christians cannot grow on a never ending "square one" gospel. Paul wearied of giving "milk" all the time. Wesley bemoaned preachers who ranted and raved about the "blood of Jesus." Our Lord quickly plunged the disciples into deeper truths, probing the mysteries of the kingdom of God. He promised that the Holy Spirit would teach us even more.

But I'm not writing this book for "sawdust trail evangelists." I'm writing to Sunday school classes in which youth and adults never have a chance to say yes. I'm pleading for churches in which conversions can occur. In your church, for example, when do you give opportunities for people to experience conversion, to make a commitment? When do they lay claim upon the Savior and enlist in his service?

John Wesley screened his ministers. His questions should be asked by every Board of Ordained Ministry about potential preachers.

Do they know God?
Have they received gifts?
Have they the graces?
Have they produced fruit?
Are any truly convinced of sin and converted to God by their preaching?

I scarcely need to remind you of churches in which an invitation to discipleship is never given, in which counseling rooms are never provided, in which the water of baptism is never administered, in which the atonement of Christ is not proclaimed, in which hands are never laid upon the heads of confirming souls, in which the sin-sick are never prayed for, in which forgiveness of sins is never experienced, in which the assurance of salvation is never felt, and in which the Holy Spirit is never received.

Here's a riddle for you: What kind of church, after thirty years of membership decline, would have downgraded its departments of evangelism and new church development to third rank levels of authority within its general boards? What kind of church would have only four or five professors of evangelism in all its thirteen seminaries? What kind of church would have a multimillion dollar apportionment to fund seminaries, but be forced to sell paintings of the apostles, graciously given by the artist, to try to fund chairs of evangelism in the remaining seminaries? Three answers are correct: (a) a church out of focus, (b) a church that has forgotten square one, (c) and a church that will continue to decline.

In trying to understand why so many churches failed to reach young adults in the past twenty years, I decided to research their music. They have never recovered from the music of the 1960s, not because of the beat but because of the message. It reflects their agony of soul. For example, Paul Stookey, of Peter, Paul, and Mary fame, wrote a song called "Hymn." He sang of going to church, light flooding through the stained-glass windows. He sang of stopping by again on Thanksgiving or

Christmas. A bald man quoted poetry and said that God was
dead, but the church would go on living. Do you recall the
poignant climax, when the old man said to the singer, who was
searching for God, "You'll never find him"?

Not find the Lord? Not in worship? Not even if you were
earnestly seeking? If Paul Stookey came into your church,
would he find God?

The Beatles were in tune with their times. They communicated with the young. Searching for life themselves, they tried
sex, alcohol, drugs, Eastern mysticism, and aesthetic breakthroughs. Adults now in their twenties and thirties and forties
were molded and shaped by the Beatles.

They wrote "Eleanor Rigby," a cry on behalf of all the lonely
people in the world, especially teenagers. Father McKinsey,
they sang, stayed up late at night, writing a sermon that no one
would hear. What was it about that sermon that made it
impossible for the Beatles (and millions of young people) to
understand, to appropriate? Did it fail to open the door for
beginners?

Eleanor Rigby died, you remember. Nobody came to the
funeral. What was it about church life that made the Beatles
believe no one would come?

Father McKinsey's sermon at the funeral had no power. "No
one was saved." The Beatles and an entire generation wanted to
be saved. But the sermons, I guess, did not connect. Was it
because young people were too far away from God, chasing
every form of self-gratification? If so, why did they write songs
about God? Did the loneliness and the mad search for life drive
them in the wrong direction? Or was it because the church had
not the passion for souls. Was it because we didn't speak their
language? Was it because the church's ears were deaf to the cry
and failed to open the door?

> Ah, look at all the lonely people!
> Where did they all come from?

Today, we need to listen to contemporary music, not so we
can wring our hands over the glorification of drugs, the
idealization of violence, or the two-beat pounding of sexual
rhythms, but so that we can hear the cries for help. Dear God,

help us hear the pleas for intimacy and relationship, the feeling of futility in a voiceless universe where nobody cares, the meaningless money mad world where, as the racetrack philosopher says, "All things considered, life is nine to five against."

Pray to God to send twenty-one-year old evangelists who can offer Christ to sixteen-year old searchers for truth in your church.

After all the experts have written all their books about the decline of historic American denominations, the answer is quite simple. Our Little Rock, Arkansas, Annual Conference last year was typical of denominational statistics: received by profession of faith 941; removed by death 1,060. Each week a few more are dying than are being born anew. Heaven's doors swing open wider than church doors do.

Our Lord said, "Behold, I stand at the door and knock; if any one hears my voice and opens the door, I will come in to him and sup with him" (Rev. 3:20). It's the duty of the church to help people, all people, find the door. Sam Shoemaker, that Episcopal priest who never tired of helping people start the faith journey, was a pastor/evangelist. He helped organize the Fellowship of Christian Athletes and led many young adults to Christ. Sam always stood at the door.

> I stand by the door.
> I neither go too far in, nor stay too far out,
> The door is the most important door in the world—
> It is the door through which men walk when they find God.
> There's no use my going way inside, and staying there,
> When so many are still outside and they, as much as I,
> Crave to know where the door is.
> And all that so many ever find
> Is only the wall where a door ought to be.
> They creep along the wall like blind men,
> With outstretched, groping hands.
> Feeling for a door, knowing there must be a door,
> Yet they never find it . . .
> So I stand by the door.
>
> Men die outside that door, as starving beggars die
> On cold nights in cruel cities in the dead of winter—
> Die for want of what is within their grasp.

They live, on the other side of it—live because they have not
   found it,
Nothing else matters compared to helping them *find it*,
And *open* it, and *walk* in, and *find him* . . .

I admire the people who go way in.
But I wish they would not forget how it was
Before they got in. Then they would be able to help
The people who have not yet even found the door.

As for me, I shall take my old accustomed place,
Near enough to God to hear him, and know he is there,
But not so far from men as not to hear them,
And remember they are there, too.
Where? Outside the door—
Thousands of them, millions of them.
But—more important to me—
One of them, two of them, ten of them,
Whose hands I am intended to put on the latch.
So I shall stand by the door and wait
for those who seek it.
"I had rather be a door-keeper . . ."
So I stand by the door.

One Monday morning, Julia and I were flying from Little
Rock to Nashville. We departed at 7:00 A.M. on the "business-
man's flight," which flies into Nashville non-stop by 7:55, in
time for a full day's work. The salespersons trooped on,
briefcase in one hand, newspaper in the other. They sat down,
buckled up, opened the *Wall Street Journal*, and waited for hot
coffee. Everything was old hat.
   Right behind Julia was a young woman who stopped at the
door of the plane. "Good morning," said the flight attendant.
"What is your seat?"
   The woman replied, "I don't know."
   The flight attendant asked, "May I see your boarding pass?"
The young woman handed her a sheaf of tickets. "Have you
flown before?"
   "No, this is my first flight," the woman said.
   "Well, you're in 11-C."
   The woman just stood there, white as a sheet.

"Let me show you where it is," the flight attendant offered. She seated the woman in 11-C. The other passengers never looked up. She helped the woman with her seat belt, then stepped into the aisle and gave safety instructions. Do you think those salespeople looked up when she told how to fasten the buckle? They were either on page two of the *Journal*, or they were already working on a sales proposal.

But the young woman listened intently. She reached under her seat for the flotation device in case we went down in the water—a rather slight possibility. Her eyes got big during the oxygen mask explanation. Do you think anyone else paid attention? No, they'd flown before. But she was on her maiden flight.

In the churches, we sing "Blessed Assurance" or "A Mighty Fortress" by heart. But some people do not know the songs. We turn to Matthew 5 or Psalm 100 or say the Apostles' Creed or the Lord's Prayer. But many people have never flown before. They know neither the words nor the music. We're talking about 40 percent of all Americans. Who will serve as "flight attendant," helping people take their very first flight?

Learning from Parachurch Groups

The soul anguished 1960s provided a fertile field for the parachurch movements. *Para* means "alongside of." That's where the kids were, alongside of the church. Kids on fire for God could hear sounds in the streets that the churches could not hear. They could speak words the churches had forgotten how to speak. They acted quickly, whereas the churches needed a quadrennial program. They offered square one religion, while the churches were spelling out the implications of the gospel or were organizing the next financial campaign.

Frank Tillapaugh was a child of the era, an unchurched boy who became a Christian while serving overseas in the army. Now, as a pastor, he assesses the strengths and weaknesses of the parachurch movements in his excellent book *Unleashing the Church*. Why, he asks, did Dawson Trotman start the Navigators during the early 1940s? Because Trotman had a burning desire to reach sailors. But why did he have to bypass denominations in order to do it? Because the churches were geared for middle income families. They were turned inward. Literature was nurture-oriented, not conversion-centered. Chaplains, by training and custom, were compassionate and tolerant of religious viewpoints. So Trotman organized a separate movement. He developed a one-to-one plan designed to invite an individual to Christ. Then he fed the new convert on a Scripture memory plan.

The denominations could not reach unchurched sailors because, in a world rapidly becoming fractured, individual, and isolated, the churches had a nuclear family mentality. He quotes the Southern Baptist Convention's *Home Mission* magazine's lament that "over ninety percent of their churches were ministering nearly exclusively to a middle class."

A long list of parachurch, evangelical groups have sprung up over the last forty years: Inter-Varsity, Navigators, Campus Crusade for Christ, Youth for Christ, Young Life, International Students, Inc., Child Evangelism, Teen Challenge, Jews for Jesus, Fellowship of Christian Athletes, and others. Why have they emerged? Because the churches could not and would not target special "outcast" groups, like kids, service personnel, college students, single adults, and athletes. They did not fit our social or theological agenda.

What strengths do parachurch groups exhibit? They're streamlined, free from the institution. Many young people fear the church, afraid they will be boxed in, their creativity inhibited. They see the church as being preoccupied with buildings and committees and budgets and parking lots. The warts and wrinkles of the institutional church are all too visible. The church seems all adult, terribly closed, and not all that exciting. E. Stanley Jones remembered that during a crusade in Japan, a student signed her commitment card, "I am 100 percent for Jesus but I'm only 50 percent for the church." A parachurch group doesn't have to carry the weight of the church on its back, like a turtle carrying its shell.

Another strength of parachurch groups is that they live in the same culture. The "friendly" middle-class family church is a million light years away from a twenty-year-old sailor who is rolling on the waves of the Pacific and whose girlfriend doesn't write. The parachurch understands the culture of the young and the unchurched. They are either "one of them," or they become "one of them."

A sixteen-year-old kid in jeans and tennis shoes wouldn't be caught dead in Sunday school, but he will hang on every word spoken by a nose guard from the Green Bay Packers who talks about Jesus Christ in football terms. The Fellowship of Christian Athletes aims at boys and girls who love sports. They speak a common language.

Why did the Wesley Foundations and Westminster Fellowships fail so miserably in the 1960s and 1970s? Because they thought incoming freshmen, products of our Sunday schools and youth fellowships, were mature Christians, eager to read Tillich and Bonhoeffer and ready to march for civil rights and in anti Vietnam protests. Reality was different. Most of the kids were uncommitted. One college president claims he saw a freshman student wandering around on campus with his umbilical cord in his hand, looking for a place to plug it in.

So the Campus Crusade asked that kid if he knew God's plan of salvation. The kid said no—can you believe that?—so a four-point plan was provided and the young man was invited into a warm friendship group of prayer, Bible study, and witness. No sacraments, no old people with blue-gray hair and silver-rimmed glasses, no children needing supervision, no institutions with societal impact, no balanced theology or biblical scholarship. But a door, a forgiveness, a simplistic faith, and a fellowship in a very cold, lonely and sin-sick world.

Another reason for power in the parachurch movement is their "hands on ministries." Not needing high powered credentials, like ordination or lay speaker's licenses, and not requiring years of training, they engage in "front-line ministries"—praying with people, witnessing, listening, studying, asking for commitments and nurturing new converts.

Most parachurch groups are not so dynamic now. Like all of us, they have gotten older and more structured. Several of them are being absorbed back into church life, mostly in conservative forms. They have many weaknesses. The parachurch organization pays a high price for its effectiveness. These churches target special age groups with an intended narrowness, but kids grow up. Tillapaugh says: "If a ministry is geared for teens, it's great while we're teenagers, but someday we all turn twenty. . . . When we in the local church reach that unchurched teenager for Christ, we don't have a transition problem."

The church is designed to minister to us from cradle to casket, not only to convert our self-centeredness into Christ-centeredness, but also to help us grow, put us to work, nourish us through life's ups and downs, feed us with the sacraments, and send us home to God amid the songs of the saints. The diversity of a local congregation is a tribute to the Christ who breaks down barriers (Eph. 2) and to the splendid diversity of the body. (I Cor. 12) "Para" groups miss the richness of the tradition and the breadth of the fellowship of the church. Some people perish, lacking spiritual nurture when their group runs out of steam. Others spend their lives looking for a church built like a group.

Churches Alive

Churches have been waking up. At first, the more organizationally flexible, more mission driven groups began to target particular populations. Then congregations of all stripes, even mainliners, began to see the needs. Churches are learning that they can minister to kids, single adults, divorced and widowed persons, artists, street people, college students, military personnel, people in jail—and do it as a functioning part of a full bodied, mission driven local congregation.

Lots of churches now are establishing singles ministries. They reach out with unique programming, social activities, therapy groups, counseling, and *Disciple* study groups, just for singles. They also integrate those same single adults into the choirs, administration, and ministry programs of the church. Singles don't have to go someplace else if they get married or grow older. They are in the faith and in the fellowship. They're family.

In good programs, an opportunity exists for square one commitment, too. Twelve single men between the ages of twenty-five and forty-five shared a *Disciple* Bible study group in one church. Several had not been in church since they were teenagers. Their comments about the study became testimonies: "For the first time I've felt the love of Christ in my heart"; "God led Moses out of slavery—I've gone six months without a drink—I feel I've been led to freedom"; "My parents dragged me to church as a kid. Now Sunday worship makes my week."

A young woman in a lesbian life-style participated in the singles fellowship. She made honest friendships of trust and left her former friends and life-style. Was it the prayers, or was it the Christian fellowship? She began to date. The pastor performed her marriage. Changed lives can still happen in the church.

If you want to see a denomination at work on the college campus, go to 25,000-student Texas Tech University in Lubbock, Texas. The Wesley Foundation there for four years has been named the outstanding student organization in the university. The Reverend Steve Moore and Amy Lerner are the directors. Here is a summary of their program.

* Over 500 students, graduate students, and faculty are involved in small group Bible studies each week, coordinated by Amy Lerner

* "Salt Shaker" leadership training equips leaders

* Lunch with a speaker once a week; faculty members and business leaders share their deepest values in a talk titled: "If I Had One Last Lecture to Give, What Would I Say?"

* Over 200 students gather each Thursday evening for singing and in-depth inductive Bible study, led by Steve

* Wesley has three to six "interns" each year—graduate students interested in entering some form of ministry, possibly student work

* Sunday evening worship service, directed by interns, student participation

* Family-style supper before service

* Opportunities for commitment, conversion, service, and life-transforming experiences

* Formal and informal counseling

* Director teaches two courses on campus: ethics and world religions; sometimes team-taught with other faculty

* Sponsors work camps in the United States and in nine foreign countries (over 300 students have participated)

* Ski trips, work projects, help at juvenile center

* An old Wesley Foundation Building, used all the time ("We're wearing it out! New experience for our conference!")

* "Come Double"—fifteen or twenty engaged couples on Friday nights to discuss Christian marriage.

As with any alive group of Christians, conversions occur. Colleges are great places for new life in Christ to begin.

How Do We Convert?

What is the best way for a congregation to make converts? Start a fresh group that will include some new unchurched people. Then turn up the heat. Give opportunities for commitment. That's why new adult classes, new Bible study groups, new women's circles, new men's prayer groups, and new youth singing groups are so important.

What's the best way for a denomination to make converts? Start new congregations. Jack Redford, an executive for the Southern Baptist Convention, has helped organize over 15,000 congregations during the past two decades. His book *Planting New Churches* is dynamite—the best on the subject. We asked Redford to talk to our Membership Growth Committee. He said that the Southern Baptist Convention would have traveled the same downhill path as other denominations if they had not started so many new churches. They have grown from 9 million to 14 million members in the past twenty years. "We need you United Methodists to start new congregations," he said. "It is the best form of evangelism. We cannot evangelize America by ourselves." Jack said, "You United Methodists have dropped from 42,000 to 38,000 congregations. If you want to double your membership, you should start 38,000 new churches." We need them. Well over 100 million Americans do not belong to any church, synagogue, or religious fellowship.

How do you start a new church? Lots of ways, of course, lots of good ways. Sometimes land is given by a developer, or a handful of laypeople begin a fellowship in a home, or a church executive does a survey, asking local people to help, or a district sends a "calling" minister to visit scores of homes in the area.

An existing congregation can "mother," or sponsor, a new church into being. "Two ways," said Redford, "colonization (sending thirty or forty people as a nucleus) or conversion. The best way is conversion. Send a converting pastor and reach out to the unchurched. New converts carry the fire of fresh enthusiasm. Sometimes the old-timers from another church may have set-in-concrete ideas, some may be misfits, some may hanker to return."

"What about money?" I asked him. "Don't you need land and buildings?"

"Sometimes," he said, "but money is not as important as pastoral leadership. Your harvest is your best resource."

"What does that mean?" I urged.

His response was, "Your converts will build their own churches. Too often we want to build a church building too soon. Let a fellowship grow for a while. They ought to be more interested in saving people than in borrowing money and laying bricks."

Too often we think we must have a half million dollars to start. We need more new congregations that keep converting people for five, ten, or fifteen years before they build a building.

"A big problem is the seminaries," said Redford. "We had to work hard to develop courses in our seminaries on how to start new congregations. Then we developed seminary courses, special workshops, summer internships, and one-year training programs for student ministers."

My thoughts raced around the world. In Africa lay preachers go out from a congregation and begin new work. Korea beats all. There are practically no church jobs for seminary graduates. A fresh Korean seminary graduate knows that he or she must start new work. Wouldn't that transform our seminaries, if every budding preacher had to convert or perish!

The United Methodist Church in the Philippines had not

grown dramatically until about 1980. Then it took off like a
jetliner, moving up from 109,071 members to 232,000 in eight
years. I asked Bishop Nacpil to explain.

> Partly it is a mystery of God. But partly it was our change in
> strategy. Before 1980 we had tried to gather money from our
> churches to the Annual Conference for church extension. Our
> churches are very poor, not much money came in, and then
> reluctantly. We didn't start many new churches. In 1980, we gave
> them their money back. "Don't send us apportionments," we
> said. "You start new congregations yourselves, for it is the
> heartbeat of the gospel."
> We cut out the bureaucracy, even the sending of "starting
> pastors." Each congregation now is supposed to send out a lay
> pastor, form a new colony of believers, make converts, and
> develop a chapel. One district had twenty-four new congrega-
> tions in 1980, but has eighty-four now and an additional eighty-
> eight outpost extension works.
> It has caused existing churches to become enthusiastic. A
> pastor and a group of laity target a nearby area or a village. They
> visit hard, working one day a week in the new area. Then they
> send a young volunteer, a young adult Christian, to work
> full-time, underwriting his livelihood. That person starts Bible
> study groups, usually in the home, then in a garage, then an
> addition to the garage, then they search for a lot and plan to build
> a building.

"Does everyone do this work?" I asked.

> "Laypeople are stepping forward to give land, large sums of
> money, real estate, or architectural knowledge because they
> believe in the work. All the conference does now is tabulate the
> results. We are making many converts. A spiritual condition
> has transformed where it is normal to be mothering new
> congregations."

I tell you it's back to basics. The book of Acts is alive in our
midst. Just as Antioch sent Paul and Barnabas to Asia Minor as
church planters, so also we must convert and cluster new
Christians.

One last thought from Redford. New churches are a strategy
for attacking the city. Is there an ethnic group that would
respond to the gospel as presented by your denomination?

What about an economic or social stratum overlooked by existing churches? As population shifts occur, are you ready to move with them? Could your congregation start a new church?

Some people say, "Oh, there are lots of churches now." They used to say that about hamburger stands. McDonald's wants to put the golden arches within a five minute drive of every American—and make money in every one of them.

Can you imagine what would happen if we had 1,000 Hispanic pastor/evangelists ready and eager to start new congregations?

Robert Burt, hard driving general secretary of the Division of Evangelism and Church Extension in the Board of Homeland Ministries of the United Church of Christ, is initiating brand new beginnings. Using this philosophy, plus relocating some churches and revitalizing others, look what his leadership has achieved. See the graph on page 117.

Right now, The United Methodist Church is hamstrung at the national division. We desperately need a fresh structure and a Robert Burt or a Jack Redford. But no matter, conferences and areas are increasing church starts. Local congregations are mothering. Bishops are helping raise money. Metropolitan areas like Atlanta, Chicago, Dallas, Fort Worth, Richmond, Los Angeles, San Antonio, Orlando, and Little Rock are strategizing.

Some ethnic groups worship in existing church buildings. First Baptist Church in Wichita has a wonderful Laotian/Thai fellowship. A Korean congregation meets in First United Methodist Church in Springdale, Arkansas. They're small, but mighty.

Renewal means that your church, if it is driven by the basic urge to fulfill our Lord's command to "go . . . make disciples" will be asking whether it can mother a new congregation without asking help from anybody but the Lord.

In Korea, one great church was not growing so much as others. Zion Central Methodist Church, located in the heart of Pusan, has a fine leader, Reverend Youngmoon Chu, who has served as pastor for over a quarter century; he is district superintendent also. I learned that as the city has grown (now

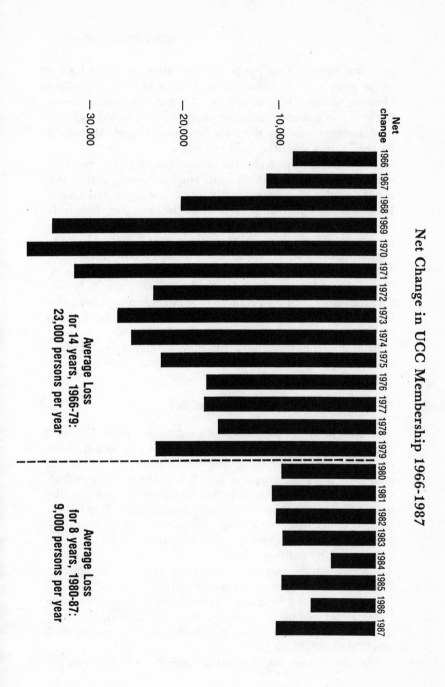

Net Change in UCC Membership 1966-1987

Net change 1966 1967 1968 1969 1970 1971 1972 1973 1974 1975 1976 1977 1978 1979 1980 1981 1982 1983 1984 1985 1986 1987

— 10,000

— 20,000

— 30,000

Average Loss
for 14 years, 1966-79:
23,000 persons per year

Average Loss
for 8 years, 1980-87:
9,000 persons per year

over four and a half million people) members keep moving out of the inner city. So the congregation sends them out with a blessing, and provides money for an organizing pastor. Across the years, as a single congregation, they have started eighteen new churches. Just like the New Testament church, they did it by themselves with the help of God.

This philosophy provides the driving force for new group life within a congregation. New adult Sunday school classes, new choirs, singles' groups, ethnic prayer fellowships, and special Lenten studies provide ports of entry for strangers. I recently talked to several pastors who receive 200 people each year on profession of faith. Many of these fledgling Christians come to commitment by way of these newly formed fellowship groups.

The approach is much like starting a new church. The key is, first of all, a Christian leader or teacher. Sometimes "colonization" can work, often with those old-timers leaving after a few months. But the leader must be someone whose faith is contagious—a lay evangelist in teacher's clothing.

Isn't this the way the Protestant Sunday school looked around the turn of the century, when our churches were growing by leaps and bounds?

Making Disciples

Starting at square one means helping people begin. We need to make converts. Once again, we must convey the call of Christ to "come and follow me." The best strategy to reach the unchurched is the opening of new fellowship groups in which commitments can be carefully and thoughtfully made. In like manner, we must start new congregations. A fledgling fellowship, with its fresh wineskins, will attract inquiries. A new congregation will baptize and confirm many who have been intimidated by existing churches.

But now what do we do? As we try to reinvent the church, looking at basic apostolic examples, what's next?

Scripture gives a clear answer. In the great commission, our Commander told us to "make disciples of all nations, baptizing them . . . teaching them to observe all that I have commanded you" (Matt. 28:19-20).

The task is now the training of disciples. Conversions are

essential, but babes in Christ must not die aborning. Recruitment of the troops is step one, but careful basic training is required.

The word *disciple* means learner. No task is more basic or more urgent than training Christians. No issue is more important than teaching converts all that our Lord has commanded. The early church "devoted themselves to the apostles' teachings," and so must we.

Disciple Training

For twenty years, as a pastor, I had been searching for a plan to deepen dedication and provide biblical grounding in my congregations. I knew we had to train the laity for ministry. That training needed to start with the Scriptures. How in the world, starting at square one, could we begin to train Christians for leadership in the local church?

We needed a doorway to help people walk into the Bible and come out disciples of Jesus Christ, ready to go to work. Where could I find an elementary plan for leadership training right in the local church?

My seminary notes told too much about the synoptic problems and not enough about the Savior's promises. Bible 101 was not what the laity wanted.

Menninger Bible Course, a splendid four-year plan, spent too much energy learning the number of jewels in Solomon's crown.

Memory plans, like Navigators, came out as literalistic, out of context, often lacking an overview of the whole Bible.

Most Sunday school curricula crawled at a snail's pace, verse by verse. Not enough was required of the student, either.

Bible Study Fellowship, lay initiated and ingenious in organizational strategy, is theologically tilted to neo-Calvinism. The involvement by tens of thousands of people testifies to the hunger for the Word, however.

Professors at the University of the South, at Sewanee, designed a four-year seminary course for laity of the Episcopal Church—solid material aimed at gifted inquiring minds.

Kerygma, a scholarly Presbyterian plan widely used in

Canada, still smacks a bit too much of J E D P theory and who wrote Mark's Gospel.

Bethel, a Lutheran plan, really helps build lay leadership. A pastor who spends two years in the Scriptures with key people who study hard is bound to wake up a church. Too much theological overlay, and not much study by participants in the congregational phase are weaknesses. Still, Bethel has turned a church around by making Bible study serious business.

Trinity gets top marks for a "you all come" study. Simple, straightforward, a minimum of overlay—Trinity can be taught by pastor or teacher to any number of people. Trinity covers the whole Bible, using a threefold approach: facts, meaning, and application. The Koreans love it because it fits a lecture style; the pastor or teacher "shoots it through his own gun." It's strength is its weakness, however. The teacher prepares more than the students do. Over 8,000 churches use Trinity in over half a dozen languages.

However, something even more powerful than any of these plans was needed. What about a design that would let the Scriptures speak for themselves? The Bible can speak to the heart as well as to the mind. The best Bible student I ever knew was an eighty-year-old construction worker's wife who had a fifth-grade education. Like the psalmist, she meditated on the Word "day and night." A good plan to help participants read the Bible—to see the whole, to feel salvation history unfold—was necessary. There should be a minimum of theological overlay, only enough professional scholarship to make sense out of the text. People should ask not so much "What does it say, and how can I apply it?" but "What is God whispering to me, and what is God telling me about my life and my world?"

I'll never forget the twenty-four hours I spent at Flower Mound, Texas, in the Episcopal Retreat Center, trying to formulate a serious Bible study to develop lay leadership. Professors Albert Outler and Dick Murray were there. So were pastors Maxie Dunnam, Ira Gallaway, and Dan Bonner. Representatives from the Board of Discipleship and from The United Methodist Publishing House shared and listened intently. Robert Feaster said the magic words: "It may cost hundreds of thousands of dollars; let's do it."

After months of preparation, after enrolling churches, *Disciple* is creating "signs and wonders" in several denominations.

Imagine a group of twelve or so, patterned after Jesus and his disciples, in which each person privately reads long and heavy passages thirty to forty minutes a day, then gathers weekly for thoughtful discussion and prayer for thirty-four weeks.

Imagine a weekly ten-minute videotape presentation with nationally known Christian teachers. How would you like to pastor a three-point charge in Idaho and team teach with some of the best preachers, theologians, and spiritual leaders in the country?

Imagine a manual guided in preparation by Dean Leander Keck, New Testament scholar from Yale, and Professor William Powers, Old Testament scholar at Perkins School of Theology, but run through the sieve of an everyday pastoral brain. Then proof it by a lay teacher who has taught under several of the plans. There are no words you can't understand.

Imagine a *required* national training program. Why, we hardly require anything in the church. It is expensive enough that a church must stop and think about it, like a called meeting to decide to fix up the parlor or remodel the parsonage. A church has to vote and enroll. Pastors have to get involved. It is a plan for training leaders and for spiritually energizing the church. *Disciple* calls the church to become again a people of the book and a community of disciples of Jesus Christ.

Imagine a plan that has quality control. All the elements of the first group of twelve are available to every other group down the pike.

In lesson thirty-three of the *Disciple* study, each participant is asked to answer the questions: What are my gifts and graces? How can I best offer them to God in and through the church? Every person is a "disciple," ready to go to work for God.

A pastor in Altus, Oklahoma, wrote an enthusiastic letter about the *Disciple* program. After participating in it for thirty-four weeks with twelve key people, he was thrilled that "the Spirit gave everyone a willingness" to work. Some offered themselves as Sunday school teachers; others now help with evangelism, confirmation, and inquirers classes. Two new teachers lead *Disciple* groups along with the pastor, so that thirty people are being trained in a second year. Together, they are rebuilding the congregation from the ground up. They are making disciples.

A thousand churches are now in *Disciple*. Two thousand leaders have been trained, and 20,000 students are working. Excitement bubbles out of individual hearts. A dentist wrote, "I had never read the Bible in its entirety. I had made attempts, but never could follow through. . . . I needed this experience in my life. I came to the realization that I could die and get to heaven, only to have God ask me, 'Did you read my book?' I figured it was time to be able to answer that question with an emphatic 'Yes!'"

One recently divorced man in his early thirties said of this group support: "God knew what I needed. *Disciple* came into my life just when I was desperate for Christian friends."

A woman in her late forties had participated in several Bible studies. "For the first time I learned how to read the Bible for myself."

In an interracial group, a young white man shared, "When we started, I didn't know how to talk to a black person. Now he's as close a friend as I've ever had."

A recovering alcoholic locked onto Moses. "This is my story," he said of Exodus. "God is leading me out of bondage into a new life."

A longtime Christian, born and raised in the church, exclaimed during Holy Communion in the final worship time together, "This is the first time I've ever experienced the Holy Spirit."

When Jesus said, "I am the true vine, and my Father is the vinedresser," he walked us right out into the vineyard. It's late fall, early winter, not spring. Unproductive limbs of the vines are being pruned away. "Every branch of mine that bears no fruit, he takes away." That cutting back is happening all over the church.

But the pruning is to get back to the basics, the essential root and vine that is Jesus Christ himself. The purpose of the cutting is twofold: to be rid of dead branches of the past that do not bear fruit and to prepare for the fresh, green fruit producing vines of the future. God prunes the church "that it may bear more fruit."

The new birth of the church requires a certain return to square one. If we can abide in Jesus "the true vine" and be faithful to his command to make disciples, we will experience healthy growth. If we can baptize in the name of the Father, the Son, and the Holy Spirit, we will be extending Jesus' mission and bringing sons and daughters into the family. If we can teach new Christians to observe everything that he has commanded, we will be fruitful. His promise is sure: "He who abides in me, and I in him, he it is that bears much fruit" (John 15:6). Jesus once indicated that there is unspeakable joy in heaven over one sinner who is converted. If we reclaim our basic work and witness, the vines will bear fruit again. "These things I have spoken to you," said Jesus, "that my joy may be in you, and that your joy may be full" (John 15:11).

CHAPTER SIX

Power

Bishop Abel Muzorewa of Zimbabwe sat down with a cup of coffee in his hand.

I said to him, "Abel, you and others have told me how Christianity has become indigenous in Africa. You've helped your country achieve freedom from colonial bondage. You've worked with missionaries who planted churches, hospitals, schools, and agriculture stations. Now the church is growing by leaps and bounds. How do you account for that?"

He looked me right in the eye and said, "God. We don't know why. We can't explain it, but God has chosen this moment in history to move mightily in Africa. We who have labored across the years can only stand in amazement and watch the signs and wonders."

Bishop Joao Somane Machado of Mozambique joined us and echoed the words. "God is behind it all. God is changing Africa. People are becoming Christians, congregations are forming, faster than we can count," he said.

We have discussed renewal. We have talked about aggressive strategies for outreach. But I ask myself, "Where does the power come from? Where will we receive the 'want to,' the spiritual drive to act?"

124

Prayer

Religion can be drier than toast. Religion can become wooden, impotent, like bleached bones in Death Valley.

After the destruction of Jerusalem, when the Hebrew people were scattered and exiles were in captivity in Babylon, the prophet Ezekiel went into his prayer closet. The Jews had no more hope of resuscitating Israel than of putting flesh on a skeleton and calling it to life. So Ezekiel prayed. Oh, how we are hurting for prophets who pray!

God grabbed hold of Ezekiel's heart and mind and lifted him in a vision.

> The hand of the Lord was upon me, and he brought me out by the Spirit of the Lord, and set me down in the midst of the valley; it was full of bones . . . and lo, they were very dry. (Ezekiel 37:1-2)

The dryness of our bones needs little additional testimony. We have money for salary increases, but not for new church starts. Our membership plunges, but we sell paintings of the apostles to raise money for chairs of evangelism in our seminaries.

Our denominational overhead goes up, and our missionary work goes down. Our youth ministries flounder, and our young people perish. The average congregation does not have a single layperson who calls week by week on the unchurched. The fire is low. The bones are very dry indeed.

As Ezekiel prayed, so also must we. Telling the church to pray may seem like urging a thirsty person to take a drink of water. But there are levels of prayer. Different ways of praying. Depths of desire.

Bishop Ki Chun Chang, while president of the Korean Council of Bishops of the Korean Methodist Church, attended the United Methodist General Conference. After one of the devotional services, when we had matter of factly prayed for the needs of the world, he said quietly, "I heard their prayers, but I did not see their tears."

Either we are not praying at all, or we are praying amiss. We are praying for the wrong things and our prayers are not being

answered. Are we praying for conversions? Are we praying that
men and women be able to say with Paul, "I live, yet not I, but
Christ, lives within me." Are we praying that God will call
Christian workers to help us? Our Lord gave us the command,
"The fields are white unto the harvest, *pray*, therefore, for
laborers." What a difference from a recruitment campaign for
clergy!

I tried to interrogate a Korean pastor about the marvelous
growth of the Christian churches in Korea. I asked about class
meetings, the biblical teaching, the establishment of fledgling
congregations. He finally replied in frustration, throwing up his
hands and saying, "You Americans are all alike; you want to
know about our *programs*, you never ask about our *prayers*."

The Korean Christians, under thirty-nine years of Japanese
domination and persecution, rose each morning for "daybreak
prayers." For an hour together, huddled in caves or huts, they
asked God for liberation. That prayer was answered.

When the Communists swept down from the north in the
1950s, the Christians rose each morning for prayers. Amid the
rubble of their cities and with artillery fire in their ears, they
prayed for freedom from the Communists. That prayer was
answered.

Is it any wonder that Christians rise for prayers at 5:00 A.M.
and assemble on Wednesday nights, on Friday nights, and on
Sunday nights for prayer? I asked Bishop Chang what they pray
for now. They pray for increased democracy. They pray for
reunification under freedom with the Koreans in the north.
They pray for the five billion people of the world who might be
won to Christ Jesus.

I recently listened to Dr. Hae-Jong Kim call us to prayer. Dr.
Kim is district superintendent in northern New Jersey for The
United Methodist Church in the United States. He under-
stands both American and Korean Christianity.

> There are different kinds of prayers and prayer life. The Korean
> Church is a "praying" church in a very special way. The early
> church prayed together as a congregation as well as individually.
> They believe in the power of prayers. The power that makes the
> church grow comes from prayer.

When Koreans pray, they always pray for the *numerical growth* of the church. Are we too sophisticated to ask for numerical growth? Do we believe in prayer life? We need to pray for numerical growth if that is what we want.

Grow is not a four letter word.

Does your congregation pray for conversions? Does your pastor pray for new disciples? Does your church pray that you might, through the power of God, help lonely people find the fellowship? Do you pray that boys and girls will be brought to God by your invitation? Do you pray that sin-sick people will find forgiveness from the Savior because of your gracious witness? In the seminaries, are you praying that you will learn how to disciple secular people? Are you praying that your church will grow?

I recall a particular daybreak prayer service in Korea. The pastor invited people to pray aloud, all together, for a few minutes. The murmur of voices became a rumble, then a roar. I was taken aback, confused, unsure. Suddenly I had a vision of kings and emperors on their thrones, trembling at the unstoppable power of a praying people. It was awesome. No wonder conversions occur daily in Korea.

That night, at yet another prayer service, I met a man from Zimbabwe. Tall and athletic, he stood out from the shorter Koreans. He was the head coach for the Zimbabwe track team during the 1988 Seoul Olympics. I asked him why he was at this worship service. His answer is a tribute to the power of a praying people: "For years I have been away from God," he said. "This morning, while I was jogging to keep in shape, one of these Koreans began to jog with me and urged me to come to this worship service tonight. So here I am." Then he said, rather wistfully, "When I go home, I must find my way back to God. There is much good I could do."

The Word

Ezekiel continued to relate his prayer vision:

[God] said to me, "Mortal man, can these bones come back to life?"

I replied, "Sovereign Lord, only you can answer that!"
[God] said, "Prophesy to the bones. Tell the bones to *listen to the word of the Lord*." (Ezekiel 37:3-4 GNB; italics added)

I have argued as forcefully as I can that the closer we are to the apostolic teachings the more nearly the course of the church will be on target. The signs and wonders of the apostles took place when they were preaching, teaching, healing, and praying. In my lifetime, I have never seen people so hungry for the Bible. I think the reason is obvious. Do you recall the experience when Jesus gave hard words to the Jews in the synagogue at Capernaum? Many took offense. Many followers "drew back and no longer went about with him. Jesus said to the twelve, 'Do you also wish to go away?' Simon Peter answered him, 'Lord, to whom shall we go? You have the words of eternal life'" (John 6:66-68).

Many people in our secular society have tried the freedoms of the sexual revolution. They have believed the cultural relativisms of the universities. They have followed the signs that point to comfort. Some have even climbed a mountain of dollars and, from the top, surveyed success. Others have fallen onto grave times because of personal tragedies. Many have gone to the broken cistern where no water is.

Lord, to whom shall we go? That is the cry of many citizens of a world flirting with madness and despair.

Let me refer again to Allan Bloom's *The Closing of the American Mind.* After a lifetime of teaching college students, he stands aghast at the lack of knowledge in university students, particularly as it relates to history, literature, and social philosophy. Instead of knowledge, they value openness, tolerance, and apathy toward value distinctions, making right and wrong seem irrelevant. The historic quest of humankind for what is good and true and beautiful is unimportant.

Students are ignorant of Socrates and Shakespeare. They do not know the Bible. Bloom writes:

I fear that an evaporation of the soul's boiling blood is taking place. . . . Today's select students know so much less, are so much more cut off from the tradition . . . that they make their predecessors look like prodigies of culture. . . . [In earlier years,] most students could be counted on to know the Bible. . . . As the respect for the latest fad has soared, real religion and knowledge of the Bible have diminished to the vanishing point.

It was the home—and the houses of worship related to it—where religion lived. Attending church or synagogue, praying at the table, were a way of life, inseparable from the moral education that was supposed to be the family's special responsibility.

How can people know the ways of God if they do not know the Word of God?

If ignorance of the Bible were a disease, public health departments would declare an epidemic.

Preachers, watch out when you're in the pulpit. If you quote David's penitential Psalm 51 or God's reply to Job, many will hear it for the first time. A quick reference to Barnabas will be lost. Only the saints will know the parables of the bridesmaids and of the wheat and the tares. Even the stories of the good Samaritan or the prodigal son cannot be taken for granted with youth, young adults, or the unchurched.

E. D. Hirsch, Jr., in his important study of reading and learning, *Cultural Literacy,* helps us to understand how children develop. Reading skills are not just like riding a bicycle. That's why "Run, Tip, Run" isn't good enough. *Content* is essential, because knowledge helps us to make connections as we read. Teachers must introduce George Washington and Abraham Lincoln in the first grade so that they can offer books on the Revolutionary and Civil Wars in the fifth grade.

So it is with the Bible. The memory work and Bible stories of early day Sunday schools laid a foundation for later Bible study. Plato was correct that specific content transmitted to children is the most important element of education.

We learn with building blocks of skill and knowledge. It is high time, in our homes and in our churches, that we offer the content of the Bible to children as well as we can, as young as we can, as interestingly as we can, as often as we can.

In Korea, Christians study the Bible, not to learn "about it," but to know how to walk as Christians. They read the Word to know the message God is revealing to them.

Each Korean Christian carries a little bag or satchel to church every time he or she goes. In the satchel are two books: a personal Bible and a personal hymnal. A wide board railing, like a minidesk, runs on the back of each pew. The worshiper comes in, opens his or her two books on the shelf, and is ready. He or she reads the Bible:

* while waiting for worship
* antiphonally and along with the lessons during worship
* in unison
* during the pastor's expository sermon
* at Tuesday Bible class
* in adult Sunday school
* during "daybreak" prayers
* for Friday night—9:00 P.M.—midnight service
* in class meetings in the home.

From Buddhism, the Koreans have a background for daily prayers and from Confucianism a practice of religious study. Conversion gives them a relationship with God through Christ Jesus. The role of sacred study requires study of the Bible for spiritual wisdom. Every new Christian knows that he or she has much to learn about the Christian God and the Christian life. They realize that the task requires a lifetime of study.

Today, Americans under the age of forty who walk into a church need to be carefully taught. A Korean Buddhist or an African spiritualist could scarcely know less about the Bible than a secular American does.

Life Changes

Miraculous things happen when people study the Bible. They put on Christ-colored glasses and see a new world.

A congregation can read "Truly I perceive that God shows no partiality" (Acts 10:34) and open their church to people of any race, age, or station.

An upper middle-class study group reads Amos, "Woe to those who lie upon beds of ivory, and stretch themselves upon couches" (Amos 6:4). So they begin to live a simpler life-style in a starving world.

"Base communities" of Latin American Roman Catholics, pushed down by economic persecution, are discovering the Bible for the first time. When they read Mary's Magnificat, governments quake: "My soul magnifies the Lord. . . . He has put down the mighty from their thrones and exalted those of low degree; he has filled the hungry with good things and the rich he has sent empty away" (Luke 1: 46-55). A revolution is on the way. God's Word will not be denied.

Two little "house circles," one in East Germany and one in West Germany, read about Jesus' weeping over Jerusalem, "If even now you knew the things that make for peace" (Luke 19:42). They begin to pray and share love offerings that will slowly tear down the Berlin Wall. Jesus spoke to us when he said, "If you continue in my word, you are truly my disciples, and you will know the truth, and the truth will make you free" (John 8:31).

The Poor

The Word is important because it takes us to Jesus, and Jesus takes us to the lost. Get close to the Savior, and you get close to the pain of the world. Jesus has an affinity for the poor.

He read from the prophet Isaiah, "The Spirit of the Lord is upon me, because he has anointed me to preach good news to the poor. He has sent me to proclaim release to the captives and recovering of sight to the blind, to set at liberty those who are oppressed, to proclaim the acceptable year of the Lord," then pronounced "Today this scripture has been fulfilled in your hearing" (Luke 4:18-19).

Ask yourself why Harvey Cox, of Harvard, states in his book *Religion in the Secular City* that modern theology has run out of steam. Haven't the churches, we "moderns," been preaching about poverty? Haven't we been commiserating over South Africa? Haven't we been pleading for racial justice?

Harvey Cox observes with insight that our theologies have, in fact, kept us from getting our hands dirty. We have become upper middle class, sheltered by our sentimental isolation. Modern theology "left out most of the people in the church and most of the people in the world. . . . It ignored the vast

populations of ordinary working men and women. . . . It for-
feited its ability to say anything to the margin."

We have been talking and preaching, but we have been
mostly sending our money away for someone else to do the job.
The power comes from "hands on," not second hand. Volunteers in mission—like doctors and dentists who serve for a week
or two in Guatemala. The Stone Soup Kitchen serves hot meals
at Quapaw Quarter in Little Rock. There is the Florence
Crittenton Home for unwed mothers. But none of these
ministries is good enough. They are good, but not good
enough, for the ultimate word is Salvation.

We insulate ourselves from the poor. In church life we isolate
ourselves from the bleeding hurts of the community. Christian
grace is reduced to almsgiving.

We have institutionalized our healing, so that even church
operated hospitals are separated from the fellowship of the
church. Food and clothing for the poor are distributed by
United Way or the Salvation Army. The destitute are distanced
from the people who gave them aid.

Power comes when the people of faith and the people in need
sit down together. Power comes when hungry souls hurt
together. Dietrich Bonhoeffer sensed in a Gestapo cell that
only by living fully in the world can we learn to have faith. Our
own salvation is at stake, for Almighty God is hard at work to
bring the whole universe together (Eph. 1:9-10).

Practical theology today is not being written in ivory towers.
It is being produced in Alcoholics Anonymous groups, where
people are being healed; in base communities in El Salvador,
where bullets whine and bread is in short supply; in college
dorms, where frightened students in sweatshirts read Paul's
Letter to the Romans and pray.

Let me warn you. There will be grinding of teeth, said Jesus.
"When you see Abraham and Isaac and Jacob and all the
prophets in the kingdom of God and yourselves thrust
out. . . . And behold, some are last who will be first, and some
are first who will be last" (Luke 13:28-30).

We sent a preacher, full of Wesleyan enthusiasm, to a small-

town church that was half-filled with the town gentry. He had
no more sense than to go calling on the blue collar workers in
the local chicken butchering plant. He started baptizing people
with eighth-grade educations who fillet chickens for a living.
Needless to say, the pastor-parish committee wanted a change
in pastors. That preacher works now in England, where he's
bringing in kids on Sunday night with guitars and contemporary music and hard-core gospel sermons. Forty, fifty, sixty
teenagers come right off the streets. Can the Methodists of
England handle that?

People who read the Bible might stumble across the parable
about the great banquet. Like the original listeners, they might
smile, as the story begins. All of us church types assume that
the invitation to the feast will come to us. Imagine their anger,
and ours, when they and we refuse. Too busy, too distracted,
too preoccupied.

So the great banquet giver sends the invitation "to the streets
and lanes of the city," not to take the Thanksgiving baskets, not
even to form daycare centers, but to "bring in the poor, and
maimed, and blind, and lame." There is still room. "Go out to
the highways and hedges, and compel people to come in, that
my house may be filled. For I tell you, none of those men who
were invited shall taste my banquet" (Luke 14:16-24).

That story helped get Jesus crucified, for it opened the doors
of heaven, leaving some of the religious people out and letting
some of the outcast people in.

People who read that story can never be content with giving
alms or making sermons. People captured by that parable are
thankful to be numbered among the blind and the poor and the
maimed and the lame, and they are eager to invite others
because it is the Savior's wish.

Fannie Crosby, the blind hymn writer, understood the story
of the great banquet. She was grateful there was room for her.
She understood that there is room for others as well.

> Now a living fountain see
> Opened there for thee and me
> Rich and poor, for bond and free,
> At the cross there's room.

The Bible can help us keep our eyes on people.

They sat me beside the guest speaker at the Chamber of Commerce dinner. I gave the invocation. The speaker was Mr. Richard Block of H & R Block Income Tax Service. I broke the ice by saying, "Mr. Block, your accounting firm is now coast to coast, one of America's great success stories. Do you do accounting for some of the large industries or banks here in the city?"

Mr. Block smiled graciously and replied:

No, we don't. Great accounting companies, those "big eight" for example, take care of the accounting needs for corporations. If you've noticed, H & R Block tries to have a little office next to a cleaning establishment or a busy little local cafe.

Every morning, when I go to my office, I picture in my mind a mother of two small children who teaches math in the junior high school. We've trained her as a tax counselor. She opens the door of that little office, sits behind a wooden desk with a wooden chair, planning to make a few extra dollars to supplement her income.

A pickup truck pulls up. A man gets out wearing cowboy boots, one pantleg caught on top of the boot. He wears a workman's cap or a western hat that, when he takes it off, shows that white line across his forehead. He wears a cotton flannel shirt, and under his arm is an old shoe box full of cancelled checks and W-2 forms. He drops that box on the bare desk and says, "Ma'am, I sure hope you can help me."

As long as we can remember that math teacher and that fellow in the flannel shirt, there will be a need for H & R Block.

As long as the church can keep people "in our mind's eye," common people, working people, poor people, there'll be a need for the church.

This book is about a church reborn. Ezekiel heard God say that resurrection of the people of faith begins with the Word of God.

Dietrich Bonhoeffer introduces his famous *The Cost of Discipleship* with these words: "Revival of Church life always brings in its train a richer understanding of the Scriptures. Behind all the slogans and catchwords . . . there arises a quest . . . for Jesus Christ himself. What did Jesus mean to say

to us? What is his will for us today? How can he help us to be
good Christians in the modern world? . . . The real trouble is
that the pure word of Jesus has been overlaid with so much
human ballast . . . that it has become extremely difficult to
make a genuine decision for Christ . . . let us get back to
Scriptures, to the Word and Call of Jesus Christ himself."

Holy Spirit

"So I prophesied as I had been told. While I was speaking, I
heard a rattling noise, and the bones began to join together.
While I watched, the bones were covered with sinews and
muscles, and then with skin. But there was no breath in the
bodies" (Ezek. 37:7-8 GNB).

It is no accident that there is tension between the fundamen-
talists and the charismatics. The rigid Bible believers have
bone and muscle, but they lack a breath of fresh air. The
charismatics go as the Spirit moves, but they lack a stable
skeletal structure. How desperately we need both Word and
Spirit.

> God said to me, "Mortal man, prophesy to the wind [*ruah*, like
> *pheuma*, meaning "breath, wind, Spirit"]. Tell the wind that the
> Sovereign Lord commands it to come from every direction, to
> breathe into these dead bodies, and to bring them back to life."
> So I prophesied as I had been told. Breath entered the bodies,
> and they came to life and stood up. There were enough of them to
> form an army. (Ezekiel 37:9-10)

All growth comes from the Holy Spirit. "I planted," wrote
Paul, "Apollos watered; but God gave the growth" (I Cor. 3:6).

> Christians were conceived in the fires of Pentecost
> Methodists were born with a warm heart at Aldersgate;
> Denominations burned with enthusiasm in the early evangelical
>   years;
> Let the Spirit burn again with us.

I believe that we are even more afraid of the Spirit than we
are of the Word. We could not hold the Salvation Army, started

by a Methodist preacher. We could not hold the Assemblies of God, started by Methodist preachers. We could not hold the Latin Methodist Pentecostals, started by Methodist missionaries.

Jesus carefully trained the disciples. He gave himself in total sacrifice. He authenticated his love in victorious resurrection. He gave the command to make disciples. But then, as the troops were ready to march, he gave the surprising order: "John," he said, "baptized with water, but . . . you shall be baptized with the Holy Spirit." Wait, he instructed them, and "you shall receive power when the Holy Spirit has come upon you" (Acts 1:5, 8).

My deepest prayer is for God to pour out fresh power in the Holy Spirit. I know we cannot demand or control God's empowering gift, even though we are so desperately impoverished. "The wind blows where it wills" (John 3:8). We cannot buy the Spirit with money. More often than not, money stands in the way. "I have no silver and gold," said Peter to the lame man, "but I give you what I have; in the name of Jesus Christ of Nazareth, walk" (Acts 8:9-13). Peter told Simeon the magician to go to hell when the trickster tried to purchase the gift.

I have been amazed to discover people experiencing the Holy Spirit in *Disciple* Bible groups. Our plan was to deepen consecrated lay leadership by grounding them in a scriptural understanding of the faith. We were not prepared for the level of faith sharing, the depths plumbed by prayer, or the moving of the Spirit in their midst.

It was a cynical non-believer who wrote for the theater of the absurd the moving drama *Waiting for Godot*. Godot never comes. The cross-like tree never spawns any form of life. But many of us testify from experience that the Holy Spirit, the power that thrusts us into mission, does comes when we "tarry."

Churches who prepare "time apart" for quiet, for prayer, and for waiting often experience the power of regeneration. Christians who retreat into marriage encounters, "celebrating marriage" weekends, ashrams, or Emmaus or Cursillo walks, often march forward again with lighter steps. They bring fresh enthusiasm into their congregational life.

The Greek word for power is *dunamis*, the root word for dynamite, dynamo, and dynamic. "You shall receive dynamite when the Holy Spirit comes upon you." That's where the want-to comes from!

Parts of faith are active, aggressive. "Follow me and I will make you fishers of men" (Matt. 4:19), said Jesus, and Matthew rose up and followed. But parts of Christianity are passive. "Wait," said Jesus, "and you will receive the power when the Holy Spirit comes upon you" (Acts 1:4, 8).

> Open my eyes, that I may see
> Glimpses of truth thou hast for me. . . .
> Spirit divine.

The more urban people become the more need they will have for quiet. High tech must be balanced by high touch. Fast paced, city activity must be countered by slow, passive listening.

Why do we plead for money from people who are not converted? Why do we cajole for church attendance with folks who have not received the Holy Spirit? Instead of saying "ought, ought, ought" to dry and dusty hearts, ought we not to help them experience the grace of Christ's Spirit?

God gives us an apostolic ministry, which many of us are neglecting. We are to receive and to convey to others the power of the Holy Spirit. The apostles laid on hands and prayed over and over again. We are given the privilege. Why don't we use it more?

When I was a young pastor, I participated in a small discussion group with several Christian physicians. To get things started, I remarked, "You doctors have it made. You can set a bone, take out an appendix, give a shot of penicillin, and see the results. You can measure your work. We pastors have to work with intangible, spiritual truths. We never can see our progress."

One tough old Lutheran physician took a deep puff on his

pipe. Then he spoke softly, but with words that jabbed me like a fist to the jaw. "How tangible, do you think, is a headache? How measurable is a virus? Besides, pastors are given tangibles to help convey God's Holy Spirit: the water of baptism, the bread and the wine of Holy Communion, the oil of healing prayer, the Holy Bible, the prayer book, and the laying on of hands." Then he looked me square in the eye and said, "Why don't you use them?"

To make disciples, we need the power.

"The promise is to you," proclaimed Peter, "and to your children, and to all who are afar off " (Acts 2:39).

Books on church growth will not save us, though they are necessary and helpful. Calling for new members as if we were recruiting for the P.T.A. will not generate spiritual vitality. You can be in the church and not be in Christ; you can be in the pulpit and not in the Spirit.

God promised the prophet Ezekiel that if these things came to pass—namely, the Word and the Spirit—Israel would be reborn. "So I prophesied as I had been told. Breath entered the bodies, and they came to life and stood up. There were enough of them to form an army" (Ezek. 37:10). Talk about a church reborn!

As a teenager, following the devastation of World War II, I was challenged to give my life to help rebuild the world. My call to preach was filled with social idealism. In seminary, with social philosophies crashing on the floor like crystal goblets and with a "don't smoke, don't drink" moralism too frail a reed to lean my life on, I discovered grace. Not just forgiveness, but the full cross-shadowed grace that accepts a child of God, no strings attached.

I began my ministry. Soon I was discouraged, working hard for results, sick with allergies most of the time. My marriage with Julia was shadowy, so that we often turned our faces to opposite walls at night. I preached forgiveness and faith and peace and racial justice and loyalty, but inside I was full of dead bones.

E. Stanley Jones gave a gentle invitation for us to surrender our lives and, by the laying on of hands, receive the Holy Spirit.

My prayer was simple. I said to God that I was weary of carrying
the whole world on my shoulders. God said that really was not
my job, anyway. God said, *All you have to do is be faithful. I'll
accept full responsibility for the course of history and the fate
of the world.* I said, "Thank you, I'm your man."

If you had knelt on my right or left, you would not have
known. But as three elders of the church, in apostolic tradition,
placed their hands on my head, I felt the world roll off my
shoulders, and I experienced an inner peace. So did Julia. The
peace was so deep, so complete that I relaxed all over. My body
experienced healing; my faith was steeled by an inner assurance; my marriage came alive again; my ministry freed up to
serve without fear of failure.

So, in our ministry—whether it was preaching a youth
revival, leading a marriage therapy group, marching for fair
housing, or collecting money for missions—we knew we were
children of God, saved by a miraculous grasp of grace and that
we are sometimes a conduit for the work of the Holy Spirit. I
figure if we could be revived by the Holy Spirit, so could whole
denominations.

Do you remember Sang Kyoo and Young Gum Lee, from the
beginning of the book, the Korean couple who wanted to start a
Korean congregation? Do you recall their prayers for power,
their plea for prayer support? Now, a few months later, they
just stepped into my office once again.

"We have twenty converts," said Sang Kyoo. "We prayed for
one lady who then had a great physical healing."

"We started three home Bible studies in three different
towns," added Young Gum. "We are growing. People are
coming from fifty miles away. God is answering our prayers."

As they spoke, I felt the mighty work of God in the church.

Walking among the dry bones, Ezekiel conversed with God.
When he prayed, it was like he was lifted into heaven. I think
the dry bones laid heavy upon his heart, don't you? Like our
forebears in the faith, Ezekiel had a hunger for souls. When
Jesus prayed for a lost world, his sweat became as blood. I hope
we will pray for the last, the lonely, and the lost until they at
least can see our tears.

God told Ezekiel that the bones would begin to move when

the Word was proclaimed. John Wesley cried out, "Oh, give me that book! At any price give me the book of God." What a moment to help the churches explore the simple profundities of the scriptures. They have the power to give life to the body.

But the wind of the Spirit, ah, that is what we need most. Where does the power to be reborn come from? It comes from God. A church trembling on the brink of new birth needs the breath of the Almighty. We cannot baptize only with water or we die. We must baptize with fire and the Holy Spirit.

It is happening here and there all around the world. God is, even in this moment, revitalizing the people of faith. God is once again bearing "witness by signs and wonders and various miracles and by gifts of the Holy Spirit" (Heb. 2:4).

This book is an excellent resource for study groups interested in understanding, celebrating, and joining God's work in the church. A videotape is also available, with leader's guide, to enhance group study (see Resources).

RESOURCES

Disciple (Becoming Disciples Through Bible Study)
The United Methodist Publishing House
P. O. Box 801
Nashville, TN 37202
1-800-251-8591 or 1-800-672-1789

Every Member in Ministry by John Ed Mathison
Discipleship Resources
P. O. Box 189
Nashville, TN 37202
(615) 340-7285

Growth Plus
General Board of Discipleship UMC
P. O. Box 840
Nashville, TN 37202-0840

Leadership Papers (a series of 12 booklets by John W. Gardner)
Leadership Series Program
Independent Sector
1828 S. Street NW
Washington D. C. 20036

Recovery of Hope
335 North Waco
Wichita, KS 67202-1158
1-800-327-2590

Signs and Wonders: The Mighty Work of God in the Church
Videotape (VHS, color, 30 min., ICN 760372)
Abingdon Press
201 Eighth Avenue South
Nashville, TN 37202
1-800-251-3320

Stephen Ministries
1325 Boland
St. Louis, MO 63117
(314) 645-5511

Volunteers in Mission
General Board of Global Ministries UMC
475 Riverside Drive
New York, NY 10115

DATE DUE

Demco, Inc. 38-293